T0058339

TALES FROM THE
MISSOURI TIGERS

TALES FROM THE
MISSOURI TIGERS

A COLLECTION OF THE GREATEST TIGER STORIES EVER TOLD

ALAN GOFORTH

SPORTS
PUBLISHING

Editor's Note:

We have kept the text from the original version, published in 2003.

Copyright © 2003, 2015 by Alan Goforth

Sports Publishing books may be purchased in bulk at special discounts for sales promotion, corporate gifts, fund-raising, or educational purposes. Special editions can also be created to specifications. For details, contact the Special Sales Department, Sports Publishing, 307 West 36th Street, 11th Floor, New York, NY 10018 or sportspubbooks@skyhorsepublishing.com.

Sports Publishing® is a registered trademark of Skyhorse Publishing, Inc.®, a Delaware corporation.

Visit our website at www.sportspubbooks.com.

10 9 8 7 6 5 4 3 2 1

Library of Congress Cataloging-in-Publication Data is available on file.

Cover design by Tom Lau
Cover photo credit AP Images

Print ISBN: 978-1-61321-717-7
Ebook ISBN: 978-1-61321-747-4

Printed in the United States of America

Contents

Part 3:
TALES FROM THE MISSOURI SIDELINES.. 161

Appendices

Introduction

Sports has been an integral part of campus life at Ol' Mizzou for more than a century. The tradition of big victories and heartbreaking losses continued through the 2001-02 basketball season, when fans were electrified by the Tigers' improbable run to the Elite Eight in the NCAA Tournament.

There is simply no better place to be on a crisp fall afternoon than Faurot Field at Memorial Stadium. Don Faurot himself, as a graduate student, helped lay the sod in 1926, and the playing surface was named after the legendary coach in 1972. It's where Norris Stevenson bravely broke the color barrier in the 1950s, where Dan Devine built a national powerhouse in the 1960s and where Al Onofrio pulled some unlikely upsets in the 1970s. Phil Bradley, Kellen Winslow and Eric Wright—household names in college and in the pros—continued to build on that foundation in the early 1980s. Hard-working players such as Corby Jones and Brock Olivo gave the program a new spark in the 1990s. And today, quarterback sensation Brad Smith just may become the best player ever to wear the black and gold.

The Tigers had little tradition in basketball until Norm Stewart returned to coach his alma mater in 1967. Big men Al Eberhard and John Brown first put the program on the map in the early 1970s; then Willie Smith electrified crowds at the Hearnes Center with his prolific scoring. Highly regarded recruits Steve Stipanovich and Jon Sundvold were the pillars of a team that won four straight Big Eight championships. Players such as Doug Smith, Anthony Peeler and Derrick Chievous took the Tigers to the top of the national rankings while rewriting the school record books. Coach

Faurot Field at Memorial Stadium
(University of Missouri Department of Athletics)

Quin Snyder has the program right on track as it prepares to move into its state-of-the-art arena.

Mizzou fans are passionate about their Tigers. Just mention the phrases "fifth down" or "4.8 seconds," and settle in for a long discussion. Missourians take pride in being known as the "Show Me" state. And for generation after generation, Mizzou athletes have shown them how to play the games with determination, passion and heart.

TALES FROM THE
MISSOURI TIGERS

1

Tales from
Missouri Basketball

The Norman Conquest

Sports figures become stars when fans know their names. They become superstars when fans know them by their first name alone (just ask Wilt, Magic and Michael).

Say the name "Norm" to college basketball fans from Ames, Iowa, to Austin, Texas, and one person immediately comes to mind—Norm Stewart, the heart and soul of Missouri basketball.

Stewart compiled a record of 634-333 as head coach from 1967 to 1999. Add in his six seasons as head coach at the University of Northern Iowa, and he retired in seventh place on the all-time victory list in NCAA Division I basketball.

His teams won 20 or more games in a season 17 times, eight Big Eight Conference championships and six conference tournament titles. His players included 28 first-team All-Conference selections, eight first-team All-Americans and 29 NBA draft picks.

Here is the most impressive statistic of all—when he retired as coach, Stewart had participated as a player, assistant or head coach in 1,127—or more than one half—of the 2,151 games that had been played in school history. No wonder there is no name more closely associated with Mizzou basketball than that of Norm Stewart.

How did a high school player from Shelbyville, Missouri (population 750) wind up starring at his state university? Credit an unlikely high school coach who had honed his craft in the basketball hotbed of Indiana.

"My high school coach, C.J. Kessler, had coached in Indiana for 19 years and had won a state championship," Stewart said. "He married a girl from my hometown whom he had met in college in Muncie, Indiana.

"Coach Kessler was a great friend of Branch Mc-Cracken, the former coach at the University of Indiana before Bobby Knight. You can imagine after coaching at both Hammond High and Hammond Tech, which is very unusual, coming to Shelbyville, Missouri. A lot of the coaches at the schools we played were not really coaches at all, but teachers who also had been assigned boys' basketball. So it was completely unfair for the other teams because of our training and everything he knew. I played in a lot of games where the score was 100-20 in our favor."

Nothing would seem more out of place to Mizzou fans than seeing Norm Stewart wearing the crimson and blue of the University of Kansas, but it could have happened.

"When I got ready to go to college, no one in our family had been to a university," he said. "I had a brother-in-law teaching at SMU, and they called. Dr. Phog Allen called, and I visited the University of Kansas. But Branch McCracken told my high school coach, 'He's a small-town kid. Send him to Missouri.' So I came to

Norm Stewart
(AP/WWP)

Missouri. I've always felt you make a decision and don't look back. It's worked out very well for me."

Stewart started 63 games from 1953 to 1956, averaging 17.7 points per game for coach Wilbur "Sparky" Stalcup. So how would Stewart, the coach, scout Stewart, the player?

"Cocky," Stewart said with a laugh. "Very self-confident. I probably was known as an offensive player. I loved to shoot it. Of course, playing for somebody from Indiana, you ran, you shot and you rebounded. Defensively, I was sound. The fundamentals and techniques came from Hank Iba and Sparky Stalcup."

Mizzou fans tend to believe that the program didn't begin to have success until the arrival of John Brown and Al Eberhard in the early 1970s. However, Stewart said, his teams enjoyed a nice run in the mid-1950s.

"As you age a little bit, each time you think back, you remember something different," he said. "But our teams really had a chance to be outstanding. Colorado beat us, and they went to the Final Four. In those days, you had to win your conference to make the tournament. The NIT didn't invite us, even though we were rated in the top five in the country.

"Some of the good games were against Kansas and Kansas State. I got to play against Coach McCracken. I also got to play against a lot of the top players in the nation."

Stewart has been a driving force behind the organization Coaches Against Cancer. Many of his former teammates have been hit hard by the disease.

"Players on those teams have had a lot of misfortunes," he said. "Lloyd Elmore and I got together and talked, and we realized we were the only people left from our team. We lost the center to leukemia. We lost Medford Park and Alva Wilfong to cancer. My roommate, Redford Reichert, died from an aneurysm."

Stewart capped his playing days by being named an All-America guard in 1956. "We won the tournament in Kansas City," he said, "but over time you first think back to the associations with your teammates and your coaches."

******

After playing with the St. Louis Hawks in basketball and Baltimore Orioles in baseball, Stewart returned to Columbia to work under his mentor, Sparky Stalcup.

"I came back as a full-time assistant in basketball and baseball and got my master's degree," he said.

"After I was here a couple of years, I wanted to be a head coach, so I started looking for jobs. Mr. Iba was very influential, and I got the job at Northern Iowa. Once I was there, I was having a lot of success and thought I could get to some other place. Somebody called and asked if I would be interested in this job. I said yes. I came down, got the job, stayed here for a long time and never moved."

******

Stewart is careful to give credit to the coaches who came before him, adding that the cupboard was not entirely bare when he arrived as head coach in 1967.

"Coach Stalcup was here for 16 or 17 years with varying degrees of success," he said. "He was a wonderful individual, and he knew the game of basketball, but as far as winning championships, we won the tournament only one time. We finished second a couple of times. Today, our ball club would have been a high pick in the NCAA tournament, but under those circumstances, we were just a ball club that finished the season and went to play another sport."

The program had fallen on hard times under Bob Vanatta, who replaced Stalcup.

"They had not won very many ball games, something like six games the past two years." Stewart said. "However, they were a ball club that was very competitive and would win a big game once in a while. Bob left a good core of people for me. They may not have been talented in terms of what we had later on, but it turned out to be a good group of individuals. I came in, sat down with the players and talked to them about loyalty and what I planned to do. We had a great three years with that group. I probably have as close of an association with them as all the others I recruited. They set the tone for the program. We stayed very competitive and started working our way up."

******

Mizzou may have been one of the first basketball programs to go with the Twin Towers theory. John Brown arrived from Dixon, Missouri, in 1971, and Al Eberhard joined the team from Springville, Iowa, a year later. The small-town players led the Tigers to the big time.

"I consider John one of my best friends," Eberhard said. "I really enjoyed being with him, on the court and off. He came from a small school also, and needless to say, he was a great player and taught me a lot about playing basketball. We helped each other in practice, and it was a great thrill to play with him. He made it a whole lot easier for all of us.

"We complemented each other on the court. We both played inside, we were strong and physical, and that was the way Coach Stewart coached basketball. A lot of our offense was geared toward getting the ball inside."

Former player Gary Link knew that group of players could turn out to be special.

"John Brown was the first really, really good player that Coach Stewart recruited," he said. "He made us all a lot better. My sophomore year, I played with Greg Flaker and Mike Griffin, who were seniors. We won 21 games and went to the NIT."

Stewart also quickly understood the potential of his young players.

"I would say when Brown and Eberhard arrived is when we started gaining some notoriety," he said. "In fact, if Bob Allen had not gotten hurt in his senior year of 1972, that might have been our best team."

The teams of the mid-1970s continued to build on the foundation that Eberhard and Brown had laid.

"After we went to the Elite Eight in 1976, everyone became our rival," Stewart said. "You get everybody's best game, and you don't sneak up on anybody. Back in the early '70s, Kansas and Kansas State were dominating the league, with Colorado having some good seasons. Then we got involved."

******

Conference games between Mizzou and K-State at the Hearnes Center and Ahearn Fieldhouse were one part basketball and one part chess match. Stewart and Wildcat coach Jack Hartman shared an intense rivalry and a deep friendship.

"I think they also were good friends, ultimately, but you would never know it," said former player Kim Anderson. "K-State always had a tradition of waiting until the visiting team went out on the floor before they went out, like 30 minutes before the game. As soon as we went out, then they would come out.

"In the 1976 or 1977 season, coach said, 'We ain't doing that tonight.' I can remember sitting in Ahearn Fieldhouse until like five minutes before the game started. Neither team would go out on the floor, and finally they broke down and went. Coach Stewart would do anything to get the edge."

As it turns out, the two coaches could hardly have been more evenly matched.

"Jack and I played each other 45 times," Stewart said. "Going into the last game, we were tied at 22-22. I tell everybody I don't know who won that final game and that it doesn't matter. But I do know who won—Missouri. I think we won as many games at his place as at ours, and he won as many games at our place as at his. We had some tremendous ballgames."

******

Who can forget the sounds of Kansas fans at Allen Fieldhouse chanting "Sit down, Norm?" Although Stewart enjoyed few things more than beating his archival Jayhawks, he also respects the Kansas program.

"When we first came in, they were so strong," he said. "Ted Owens had such outstanding teams. The first time we played them, we went over there and won a game with two free throws after the horn went off. We were down by one, got fouled with a one-and-one, made them both, and we won the game. That made it interesting from that point on.

"Kansas always has had great teams, good traditions and great coaches. I always wanted to do a little bit better job of getting our fans to understand the game so they could appreciate such things as the officiating, the teams and the other coaches. You have to be sportsman-like with the competition, and overall, KU has done a good job of that. They have had their moments when things have happened, and so have we. But it has been a good rivalry."

******

If Brown and Eberhard were the foundation of the program's success, the arrival of Steve Stipanovich and Jon Sundvold in the late 1970s was the next great coup. The plans for recruiting the highly touted center from St. Louis and guard from Blue Springs, Missouri, were as worthy of Norman Schwartzkopf as Norm Stewart.

"We sat down in our staff meeting and developed a plan to recruit both of the players," Stewart said. "We had been in association with Stipanovich, because we previously had Jim Kennedy and Mark Dressler from his high school. His coach, Rich Grawer, was a great friend and one of the best high school coaches ever in this state.

"We set up a book and included every angle. We followed a plan and inserted things as we went along. It was a very well-planned recruiting effort, and it involved marketing, public relations and everybody from politics through education."

The success of the plan carried the Tigers to greater national prominence and an unprecedented four consecutive conference championships during the Stipanovich-Sundvold era.

"Obviously, it was successful, and they gave a lot of people a lot of great basketball and great times," Stewart said. "They were great guys, and they still are. The university is proud of them, and they are proud of the university."

******

Fans who remember Stewart pacing the Tiger sidelines may have trouble envisioning him cutting loose
and having a good time. But not Jim Kennedy, who
played for the Tigers from 1974 to 1977.

"The most enjoyable times we had were away from
the game," Kennedy said. "The beginning of our junior
year, Norm decided to take the guys on a float trip. A
lot of the guys from the city had never been on water,
and half of them couldn't swim. I remember our trip
down to southern Missouri, sitting in the front seat
of Norm's Cadillac and him pulling out a big cowboy
hat, putting on country and western music and singing
along to the radio.

"The experience we had as a team on that float trip
was one of the more special moments we had as a group,
to see him away from the game. We got a lot of good
laughs out of that trip."

******

Few people are closer to Norm Stewart than Kim
Anderson, who played for him from 1974 to 1977 and
later coached under him. Even longtime fans don't fully
understand Stewart and what he has meant to the state,
the university and his players, said Anderson, now the
head coach at Central Missouri State University.

"I don't think people really know him," he said.
"He obviously was good at coaching the Xs and the Os,
but the thing he taught me and a lot of guys is how to
survive, more off the court than on. My father was a
great influence on me, and coach is a great influence."

"Coach Stewart had a method to the madness. I've often thought, after I've coached with him, wouldn't it be neat to coach with him first, then go play with him? Then you would have a great understanding of what he was doing. He had high expectations. There were a lot of things he taught you that didn't have anything to do with basketball. I can remember him getting on my rear because I didn't shave, or I might show up looking like a bum one day. Surprisingly, now that I am coaching, that all carried over. I do the same things with my guys now.

"I think about playing for him, and it was tough. But you know, it made us tough, and there was no situation we weren't prepared for. I don't know if it's that way with today's kids. Some of them have never been pushed. That's something I appreciated, that he pushed me. He pushed me in basketball, he pushed me in class, he pushed me off the court. A lot of that has to do with my own upbringing, but he reinforced that.

"Did I love him every day? No. But I respected him, and that continues today. He came to four of my games this year. He didn't have to do that. If you're loyal to him, he's going to be loyal to you and do anything he can to help you. But if you are not, then get ready for a battle."

The competitive fire is always burning, Anderson said. "The persona of Coach Stewart is misleading sometimes," he said. "He is really competitive. If you get on an airplane and play cards with him, you'd better bring your 'A' game. If you're his partner, you'd better be on your 'A' game, too. He's always on his 'A' game.

If you go out to the golf course, you'd better be ready on that No. 1 tee box. He always finds a way to win, and that's something he taught us.

"Yeah, he taught me all the basketball stuff—but he did so much for his players that he never really got recognized for. The guys who hung with him, to a man, will say the same thing."

Guys like Al Eberhard, for one.

"You were just so disciplined mentally," he said. "It came from how tough Coach Stewart was, both mentally and how tough he played. That philosophy certainly came across, and it made us better players and better people."

******

Stewart, for his part, has no regrets about his rich legacy at Mizzou.

"I feel pretty comfortable with what I have been able to do," he said. "Like anybody else, I would like to have done more, but a guy told me one time there's not much behind us, it's all in front of us."

"I'd like to be remembered as a good coach. I didn't cut any corners, I kept my family in focus, and I included the players in my family. I tried to do a good job for the university and for the people in the state of Missouri, and I still try to do that."

A Pillar of the Program

Al Eberhard averaged 16.8 points per game from 1971 to 1974 and became a first-round draft pick of the Detroit Pistons. Freshmen were ineligible when he joined the program, but he stepped in as a starter in his sophomore season and went on to start 80 games.

"The thing I am most proud of is the fact that Coach Stewart put enough confidence in me that he started me as a sophomore," he said. "He taught me so much. Just the fact that he had confidence in me to put me in the starting lineup was the biggest thrill I could ever have hoped for."

******

Eberhard teamed with John Brown, who was in the class ahead of him, to provide the best one-two punch in school history to that point. The team enjoyed success from the outset.

"We won the Big Eight Christmas tournament all three years, and that was always a meaningful tournament," he said. "When I was a sophomore and John Brown was a junior was the first time we had won it in years. It was that tournament where our program took a giant step forward. My first two years, we went on to go 21-6. That first Christmas tournament we won, we proved a lot to ourselves."

But it was an 83-79 loss at Kentucky that served notice that the Tigers were a force to be reckoned with.

"Adolph Rupp was still coaching, and the Wildcats were highly thought of," Eberhard said. "We played them the first game in a four-team tournament and lost, but we had the opportunity to win. For the University of Missouri to go down there and be competitive with the University of Kentucky was surprising to some. I think we proved a lot to ourselves and to the nation. We made a statement.

"The next year we went down to Tennessee, which also was highly ranked. I don't think anyone had ever won at their place in their tournament. We played really well for a couple of games and won that tournament. In my junior year, we were ranked as high as fifth in the nation."

Teammate Gary Link remembers something else about the Volunteer Classic, where the Tigers were supposed to be a sacrificial lamb.

"Quite frankly, they didn't invite teams down there to win," he said. "Things were set up for the home team to win. What they planned to do before the game was darken the gym, put a spotlight in the huddle, introduce John Brown, shine the spotlight on him and he would run out. But as soon as the gym went black, Coach Stewart told all five starters to scatter. He said, 'Run.' So they introduced John Brown, put the spotlight in our huddle and he wasn't there. They tried to find him, then introduced the next starter, and he would be somewhere else. Before the game ever started, the people were booing, screaming and hollering."

The Tigers upset the Volunteers and won the championship, 67-57.

******

Eberhard is proud that he and Brown set the tone for the ongoing success of the basketball program.

"I owe Coach Stewart a ton of gratitude for what he did for my basketball career, but he also taught me how to be a better person, and that was the most meaningful thing he did," he said. "He took a lot of us with raw talent, refined it, put it in a structure and we ended up being pretty successful with him. When you play the Tigers, you had better be prepared to play every minute of the game, because the University of Missouri is going to play harder than anyone you have ever played. I hope I am remembered as somebody who played as hard as he could every second he was out there and was a great representative of the University of Missouri.

"I was just thrilled to be able to play for Coach Stewart and be a part of a great program and come away with a college degree from a great institution."

A Link to Success

Gary Link was a key recruit as Norm Stewart built the Tiger program in the early 1970s. He was a blue-collar player who came to typify the program, playing tough defense and sacrificing his body for a rebound.

"Most people would say I was an overachiever," he said. "I was not very physically strong, but I had a knack for the basketball. I thought I played really good defense. The reason I was on the floor more times than not was that I played solid defense."

"The biggest compliment I ever got from a coach was that I never tried to do something I wasn't capable of doing. I realized my limitations in a positive way. I knew what I could and couldn't do. I was six-foot-five, and back then that was good enough. I played with the physical ability I had, but I tried to use my head and figure out where the ball was going to go."

Today, Link is a color commentator on Mizzou radio broadcasts. He has had a courtside seat to the great moments in Tiger basketball for more than three decades. Growing up in St. Louis, he always had his heart set on becoming a Tiger.

"I always hoped that if I was good enough to play college basketball, I would be good enough to play for my home state," he said. "That was very special. The fact that Norm Stewart was here made it even more special. He was just kind of getting his program started then.

I had scholarship offers from a lot of other schools in the Big Eight and some in the Big 10, but as soon as Coach Stewart and Mizzou came calling, I knew this is where I wanted to play."

******

Link and Eberhard enjoyed success from their early days on the freshman team through their senior season.

"Al and I played on the freshman team," he said. "In my sophomore year, some people thought we could win. In my junior year, we were expected to win. And in my senior year, people thought we would finish seventh the conference, but we won. Al and I were co-captains in our senior year.

"We won the Big Eight Christmas tournament in Kansas City three years in a row. That hadn't been done before, and it hasn't been done since."

******

Link was one of a handful of players to compete both in intimate old Brewer Fieldhouse and the sparkling new Hearnes Center. Both were great environments for college basketball, he said.

"Al Eberhard and I were fortunate enough to play the last game in Brewer and the first game in Hearnes," he said. "Hearnes opened our junior year, and we had a chance to play in both. That was special. Brewer Fieldhouse sat about 4,000 or 5,000 fans. You get a chance to play in a brand-new building, and back then, it was one of the best arenas around. I may get a chance to broadcast the last game in Hearnes and the first game in the new arena, and that way I can say I was in three different arenas."

******

Link was involved in many of those epic games between Missouri and K-State.

"They were great games," Link said. "If I hadn't gone to Missouri, I probably would have gone to K-State. Jack Hartman was at Southern Illinois University-Carbondale when he had Walt Frazier and those good teams down there. I was really impressed with Jack Hartman, one of the class guys. I enjoyed playing against him all four years at Missouri, and we stayed in touch."

Link frequently was matched up against Lon Krueger of K-State, who went on to coach his alma mater, Florida, Illinois and the Atlanta Hawks.

"He and I were freshmen together, so I got a chance to play against him all four years," Link said. "Lon was just a great player, a class guy and later a successful coach. Those games were the way basketball was meant to be played. We played hard and physical, but there was never one thing that was even borderline dirty. It was so physical, but after the game, Coach Hartman and Coach Stewart would shake hands, we would shake hands with their players and there was a mutual respect that I didn't have for anybody else. We were very evenly matched, and the coaches mirrored each other. Both teams played the game the right way."

So did the coaches.

"Coach Stewart was a master at taking the crowd out of the game," Link said. "He said, 'You fellows worry about Lonnie Krueger and the good players out there, and I'll take care of the coach and the crowd.'

"When you were on the floor, there were a lot of teams that had more talent than we did, and that's why we lost games. But we never got outcoached. Coach Stewart worked as hard as any coach I've ever been around, and he gave us every opportunity to win. We never made it to the Final Four for him, but it wasn't because Coach Stewart never gave us the opportunity. We just weren't quite good enough."

******

Who would Link place in his starting lineup for an all-time Tiger team? It's not an easy decision.

"Jon Sundvold and Steve Stipanovich for sure," he said. "John Brown and Derrick Chievous. Then Doug Smith, Anthony Peeler or Willie Smith —you couldn't go wrong."

What about Gary Link? He should merit at least a reserve role.

"I hope people would say, 'Gary Link gave it everything he had,'" he said. "In every game, win or lose, you got an honest effort. I'd like to think I gave as close to 100 percent as I could every basketball game, because I don't believe in that nonsense about giving 110 percent. I hope people realize that Missouri name on the front of the uniform meant an awful lot to Gary Link. Every time I put that uniform on, it was a privilege. I never took that lightly, and I hope I represented the guys who came before me and went after me as well as I could."

Building on the Foundation

Kim Anderson, first and foremost, is a student of the game. That may be one reason why the Big 12 Conference tapped him to be its first director of basketball operations. Serving as an assistant coach under Norm Stewart and now as head coach at Central Missouri State University gives him a broad perspective to look at the development of the Missouri program.

"The John Brown-Al Eberhard group took the program to a competitive level," he said. "We took it one step higher, into a championship level and the final eight, and maybe a little more national prominence than what they got with John and Al. Those were the guys who set the table, and I've always had a great deal of admiration for them. They were guys who got it started, and we were able to build on it. Our era was a group of guys who were able to win the first championship for Coach Stewart, and that was a great satisfaction.

"Then Jon Sundvold and Steve Stipanovich took it to the top, and it has remained there for quite a while. For the most part, the program is always competitive and challenges for a tournament berth. The core of this program under Coach Stewart was always Missouri kids. There were always two or three guys from Missouri who mirrored the coach and the way he used to play. I think coach loved those guys. I know he did."

Anderson, who grew up in Sedalia, Missouri, without question was one of those players.

"I grew up a fan of Norm Stewart and the University of Missouri," he said. "I had gone to Coach Stewart's camp when I was in seventh or eighth grade, and Missouri is where I wanted to go. But like a lot of kids, I got caught up in the recruiting process, and I visited Kansas, Kansas State, Texas, Vanderbilt and Memphis State. But I think deep down, Missouri is where I always wanted to go, and my decision was not a hard one. It was a very good one for me."

******

Anderson joined the team in 1974 and helped it clear the next major hurdle, a Big Eight championship.

"My best memory was in 1976 when we won the championship," he said. "We went to Manhattan to clinch a tie by beating K-State [81-72], then ended up winning it outright the next game. Because it was something that hadn't been done for a long time, it just meant a lot to the program. I remember the overall excitement of winning that championship, the locker room after the game, the tremendous sense of accomplishment and coming home and having the people meet us at the airport. That was a time when the program elevated itself to a different level."

The season didn't end with the conference championship. The Tigers also went deep into the NCAA tournament.

"I think the game that will stand out in my mind is when we went to the final eight in 1976," Anderson said. "We played Michigan, and it was the night Willie

Smith scored 40. Michigan had a great team, and we actually led with five minutes to go, but they came back and beat us [95-88].

"We had opportunities to go to the Final Four, and at the time I can remember talking to coaches and some of the guys who were coming back and thinking, 'Well, we'll just come back next year.' You know, it's hard to do that. We've often talked about the opportunity we had, and we didn't quite get over the hump. It's a very narrow window, and you just don't come back next year. There are so many factors that get involved."

******

The Kansas Jayhawks were replacing the K-State Wildcats as the No. 1 rival when Anderson played.

"If I had to pick one thing, I had a great satisfaction from scoring 38 against Kansas one time at Hearnes," he said. "I remember when I was a freshman that we went over to Lawrence, and KU beat us extremely badly, by 30 points maybe. It was a season where we struggled, and I know the next year they came to Hearnes, and we beat them by 30. That was a great satisfaction for us, to be able to turn that around. The Kansas-Missouri rivalry has always been great. At that time, the Missouri-K-State rivalry maybe was not quite as intense but almost as close."

******

Team chemistry can be as important as individual talent when it comes to winning championships. Anderson remembers the special camaraderie among his group of players.

"They were all good guys," he said. "We had a core group that came in when I was a freshman. At that time, there weren't scholarship limitations, and it seemed like we had 25 guys on some form of scholarship. Through the normal rates of attrition and kids moving on to other interests, when we got to be seniors, it was me, Scott Sims, Jim Kennedy, Danny Van Rheen and Jeff Currie.

"The five of us hung together over a four-year period from when we weren't very good to where we had good teams. Willie Smith came in and obviously was a huge factor, and Clay Johnson joined the team our senior year, but our core group stuck together from day one. We had some ups and downs, but it was fun to go through it with those guys."

******

Anderson played his entire career at the Hearnes Center when Mizzou basketball became a hot ticket. He has long appreciated the strong fan support.

"There has always been a great core of fans at Missouri, and I can remember 5, 6 or 7,000 people. Then, as we got better, more people came to watch us. The program wasn't at the level it was when I left as an assistant in 1999, but I think there has always been a great group of fans, and I've always appreciated those people. I think Missouri fans are great fans. They are intelligent fans, and they get behind their team. It was a period of growth when I was there as a player, and it kept on growing."

Fitting the Mold

Jim Kennedy may not have been the first hard-working, hustling Missouri kid to play for Norm Stewart, but he fit the description to a T. He also was the first in a pipeline of players from DeSmet High School in St. Louis, which also produced Steve Stipanovich.

"I would like to be remembered as part of the profile of the Missouri-type player," said Kennedy, who played for the Tigers from 1974 to 1977. "I like to think I was somebody who represented the university well, who was an unselfish guy, a guy who was team-oriented, hard-nosed, played every night and fit a certain tradition or profile that was established back in the late '60s and early '70s that really was an extension of Norm. Most teams are extensions of their coaches. In many respects, I think that profile will stand forever and is part of the success they are having today."

The transition to college was easy for Kennedy because of the similar styles of Stewart and his high school coach, Rich Grawer.

"I played for Coach Grawer for a couple of years, and they have a lot of similarities in how they approach the game," he said. "I think they both had a good balance between the basketball issues and the non-basketball issues."

******

Fans can thank Stewart for persuading Kennedy to come to Mizzou—Virginia Stewart, that is.

"Norm and Virginia seemed to really click with me and my parents," he said. "They went out and had some good times, and I was impressed."

******

Kennedy was part of the Kim Anderson team that brought Stewart his first Big Eight championship.

"Winning a championship had never been done before, despite all of the close second-place finishes," he said.

"The manner in which we had to do it, in terms of going to K-State to have to win a game, was a great achievement. My memory is playing at old Ahearn Fieldhouse, which was just incredibly challenging. It was not one of the new modern arenas. It was really old-style basketball and a small-town atmosphere. The crowd really was right on top of you.

"We were going up against one of the finest college coaches ever to coach the game in Jack Hartman. He got so much out of his team. To beat him anywhere was always a challenge, but it was something to beat him in their place in a year where they had quite a club. They were very skilled, and I just remember after the game the tremendous feeling of achievement."

A loss at another legendary arena also stands out to Kennedy from that season.

"We played UCLA at their place earlier that season," he said. "For anyone raised within the basketball environment, being able to play at Pauley Pavilion was a thrill for me. It wasn't really one of my more productive games, but in terms of a memorable game, it was just a thrill to go onto their floor and play against the dynasty it was back then."

UCLA won the game, 83-71.

Four Straight in the Big Eight

Steve Stipanovich may have been the most highly sought-after recruit in the history of Missouri basketball. Norm Stewart and his staff developed an elaborate strategy to entice him to Mizzou, while Rich Grawer, his high school coach, tried to shield him from overzealous recruiters.

Stipanovich himself, however, enjoyed the process.

"It was interesting for me, because I was heavily recruited by a lot of colleges around the country," he said. "Back then, you could choose six recruiting visits, and my six choices were Duke, North Carolina, Kentucky, Notre Dame, UCLA and Missouri. They all were top programs.

"I don't remember looking at Missouri as a program that had not had any success, because it did have success under Coach Stewart previously. But it was more of a football conference back then, and I was looking at schools that were some of the top programs in the country.

"I took five of my visits before my senior season ever started, then I visited Mizzou after the season. It was a battle. Missouri obviously recruited me very hard. Coach Stewart and the rest of the coaching staff were around a lot during the times they could talk to me. I was well protected, and the recruiting trips were a lot of fun. After I took my recruiting visit to Missouri, I realized it was the best place for me to go."

Former Tiger Jim Kennedy played a role in his decision.

"Jim was kind of a role model for me, because he went to the same high school," Stipanovich said. "He was three or four years older than I was, and we all looked up to him."

Stipanovich more than lived up to his advance billing. He helped lead the Tigers to four consecutive Big Eight championships from 1979 through 1983. He was the conference Newcomer of the Year in 1980, All-Conference in 1982 and 1983 and Player of the Year in 1983. After his senior season, he also was named a consensus All-American and a first-team academic All-American. He left Mizzou with career marks for scoring, with 1,836 points, and rebounding, with 984.

But perhaps the best tribute to Stipo was the way opposing coaches had to adjust to the seven-footer's dominating presence in the middle. He was the first in the wave of outstanding Big Eight centers, including Wayman Tisdale at Oklahoma, Dave Hoppen at Nebraska and Greg Dreiling at Kansas.

"A lot of people say I am responsible for changing the recruiting process in our conference," he said. "A lot of the opposing coaches have told me that when I came to Missouri, they all of sudden had to go out and focus on recruiting bigger centers to combat me."

******

The names of Steve Stipanovich and guard Jon Sundvold are forever linked in the memories of Tiger fans. The two players nearly met in the Missouri high school playoffs.

"We almost met in the state tournament my senior year, but Blue Springs lost," Stipanovich said. "If they had won one more game, we would have played them, which would have been fun.

"In our senior year, Jon and I went to a couple of Mizzou games together. I was more of a nationwide type of player, while Jon was a great player but wasn't as heavily recruited out of high school. We talked a little bit before we each made our decisions. It boiled down to Missouri or Notre Dame for me. I chose Missouri, and shortly after, he did as well."

******

As it was for Kennedy, the transition to Missouri was easier because of the similarities between Stewart and Grawer. Grawer went on to become an assistant coach at Missouri and later, head coach at St. Louis University.

"They both stressed hard work and fundamentals," Stipanovich said. "That's what I needed as a big guy, someone to push me physically and teach me the fundamentals of the game. That's how both those guys coached. It was a good fit for me. They helped me get ready for the next level, the NBA."

Stipanovich was the No. 2 overall pick in the 1984 draft and played five seasons for the Indiana Pacers before an injury ended his career.

******

The tandem of Stipanovich and Sundvold enjoyed immediate success.

"My freshman year, we beat Notre Dame in the NCAA tournament [87-84 in overtime]," Stipanovich said. "It was an upset. They had Kelly Tripucka and Orlando Woolridge and a great team. They probably overlooked us, and we played a great game. That was a big win for us. I also remember my freshman year going up to Illinois, when Larry Drew was a senior. We won in overtime [67-66], so that was a big win for us."

The Tigers compiled a 5-3 record against Kansas when Stipanovich played.

"Kansas wasn't the powerhouse that they have been for the past 10 years or so, but they had good teams," he said. "They had a great program, and Norm Stewart did everything he could to foster a rivalry for the players. It was a great rivalry. It's tough to go into Allen Fieldhouse and win."

About the only regret Stipanovich has about his playing days is falling short of making the Final Four.

"The best memories were winning the four Big Eight championships," he said. "I think we won over 100 games in four years. It's always fun to win. At the same time, we never got to the Final Four. It was disappointing, because a couple of those years, we were good enough to make the Final Four and didn't. That's how great coaches and teams are measured."

******

Stipanovich had the opportunity to match up against many of the best big men in the nation.

"We played Georgetown with Patrick Ewing—that guy was a physical specimen," he said. "Hakeem Olajuwon was at Houston, and they ended up beating us [79-78] in the NCAA tournament. We played that year in the old arena in St. Louis. If we had beaten Houston and Boston College, we would have gone to the Final Four. That was the most disappointing moment of my career."

******

Stipanovich gave the Tigers everything he had, game in and game out.

"I really felt I played to the best of my abilities," he said. "People are blessed with a certain amount of talent, and I think through my hard work and the coaching staff there, I was able to realize all of my potential.

"A lot of players don't do that. A lot of players that I have played with in the pros and in college have so much talent, but they never live up to their full potential. They get by and are successful, but boy, if they just worked harder and took it more seriously, they would be that much better of a player.

"I can look back and always say to myself that I worked hard and got the most out of my God-given ability. I was able to be in the NBA for five years and would have played a lot longer if I hadn't gotten hurt. I was the starting center for the Pacers. Any coach who has ever coached me, from Rich Grawer to Norm Stewart to a couple of coaches in the NBA, have always said the same thing, that I was a pleasure to coach and that I did everything the coaching staff ever asked of me. I worked extremely hard."

******

Steve Stipanovich and Jon Sundvold brought the Tigers to a national prominence the program had not experienced before, and for the most part, they have remained there in the two decades since.

"I came to Missouri very highly recruited," Stipanovich said. "I don't know if I lived up to people's expectations or not, but no one ever questioned my hard work and my dedication to improving myself as a basketball player. I don't know if Jon and I are remembered as maybe taking Missouri basketball to the next level, but since we played, they definitely have done well."

Mizzou's Cal Ripken

Mizzou basketball has always been less about superstars than about individual players who knew their roles, accepted them and played them to the best of their abilities. Perhaps no one was more of a consummate team player than Mike Sandbothe.

"I think you need some role players on the team," he said. "There is only one basketball. It's great to have five guys who can score, but you also have to have someone doing the little things. You still have to rebound the ball, someone has to set a pick, someone's got to make a pass. I think we were all real team players back then. Of course, we had an outstanding player in Derrick Chievous. I'm thinking, 'Should I shoot or give it to Derrick?' It was pretty easy to determine who had the best chance of making it."

Between 1986 and 1989, Sandbothe played in more games—134—than any player in team history.

"I came ready to play every night and did whatever it took to win," he said.

"I always had to guard the toughest guy on the other team, whether he was six-foot-10 or six-foot-two. My role was to make everybody else play better."

******

Before he got to Mizzou, Sandbothe met a player who could have been one of the all-time greats but died a tragic death.

"I also visited USC," he said. "It was the first time I had ever been on a airplane. I actually was on the same recruiting trip as Hank Gathers. He went to USC for two years before he went to Loyola-Marymount. I hung out with him the whole time."

Gathers collapsed on the court in the first half of a March 4, 1990 game against Portland. He died two hours later.

******

Sandbothe did the things that often don't always show up in the box score. Looking back, he believes he could have scored a few more points.

"If I had it to do over again, I would shoot the ball a lot more," he said. "When I came in as a freshman, I had more confidence in my rebounding, my defense and my assists. Those were things I knew I could do well. When you start as a freshman, as I did, those are the things I was confident in. It wasn't like I sat on the bench two years and then started playing. I got into that role my freshman year, and it was hard for me to get out of it. I stopped looking for my shot as much and became more of a role player. But as long as we won, that's what mattered."

******

Sandbothe enjoyed the challenge of big games and going against elite players. More often than not, he rose to the occasion.

"I always had to guard Danny Manning when we played Kansas," he said. "I had to guard him at Missouri as a freshman. He came up and started talking to me—not bad talk but just pleasant conversation. He was just a really nice guy. That threw me off.

"I also remember a game at Oklahoma State where I scored the winning basket off a Derrick Chievous miss. That was kind of nice. I would like to have beaten Syracuse in the Sweet Sixteen to go to the Elite Eight, but we didn't quite get it done.

"I remember beating UNLV at UNLV when we were heavy underdogs, and we beat North Carolina in the preseason NIT. Those were two games that stick out for me, and of course, Kansas victories are always nice. I was 4-0 against Roy Williams in the years I was there."

******

Sandbothe grew up in a family with seven children and a no-nonsense father. That prepared him well for playing under Stewart.

"Coach was kind of like my dad," he said.

"My dad expected us to do things, and you didn't ask. I was kind of brought up that way, My dad also was a coach for awhile and a high school principal.

"One time Norm decided for whatever reason that I drank too much water during practice. We had about a three-hour practice, and he tells me 'Sandbothe, that's it. No more water for you.' Everyone goes to the water jug, and I just have to stand there. I'm about to faint, because I've had no water. I sneaked behind the goal and got a water bottle that had just a little bit in it. So I'm squirting it in my mouth and all of a sudden it reaches the bottom and makes that squishy noise.

"Norm ran over there, grabbed the bottle and threw it to the D section. He literally kicked me in the hiney a couple of times and kicked me out of practice. He made his point. I had to go to the trainer's office. He said, 'This guy has to drink water, because he sweats a lot.' Norm called me a couple of names and said, 'OK, get out there and practice.'

"You don't really appreciate Coach Stewart until you get out, but I think he was a good coach and did a lot for Missouri."

******

Students of the game were more likely than casual fans to appreciate Sandbothe's style of play. One of his highest compliments came from an unlikely source.

"Whatever it took to win, that's what I tried to do," he said. "But that's not where you always get the glamour, playing the defense and setting the screens. Only people who really appreciate basketball understand that. I remember Roy Williams came up to me one time and said I was one of his favorite players who played at MU."

The Gentle Giant

Detroit has long been fertile ground for Mizzou recruiters, from the days of Nathan Buntin and Lee Coward to Ricky Paulding and Arthur Johnson. But perhaps no Motor City player has left a bigger mark on the program than Doug Smith.

Playing from 1988 to 1991, Smith led the Tigers to a 94-35 record, a conference championship, two post-season championships and three NCAA tournament bids. He was the third player in league history to score more than 2,000 points and grab more than 1,000 rebounds. Smith was conference player of the year in his junior and senior seasons and a sixth-round draft pick of the Dallas Mavericks.

But the best memory of all was having his No. 34 jersey retired after coming back to play his senior season. He joins former Tigers Jon Sundvold, Willie Smith, Steve Stipanovich, Norm Stewart and Bill Stauffer in that elite group.

"I had a great time coming back for my senior season," he said. "We all sit around and think what would have happened if I had come out as a junior, but I have no regrets going back to school. I accomplished a lot of things with the young guys and had a lot of fun doing it.

"Just the opportunity to be a student athlete at Missouri was great for me. The best moment was my last game as a senior coming back and having my jersey

Ricky Paulding
(Getty Images)

retired right after the game. That was a really, really special moment. The all-time leading scorer, Derrick Chievous, doesn't even have his number retired. That's a big deal for me."

******

The Tigers and Kansas Jayhawks swapped No. 1 national rankings several times while Smith played, and he relished their epic battles.

"We beat them, then they would beat us," he said. "Oklahoma was right there with us. We had three of the top five schools in the nation."

Smith finished his career as the No. 2 scorer in school history, with 2,184 points. He knew how to find the basket.

"One game, I had 44 points against Nebraska, which I think is the all-time record in Hearnes," he said. "I had the opportunity to set the school record, but I'm not all that concerned about records. The next week, I had 72 points in two games."

The Tigers were on probation his senior year and ineligible for postseason play. Smith and his teammates made a statement, however, by making the conference tournament in Kansas City their postseason.

"The thing that sticks out is when as a young basketball team with all those freshmen my senior year, we went and won the Big Eight tournament," he said. "We already knew we were on probation. That team could have gone a long way in the NCAA tournament, but hey, we didn't get a chance to do that, so we just tried to use the Big Eight as our tournament."

******

Smith and roommate Anthony Peeler gave the Tigers one of the best inside-outside threats in college basketball.

"Anthony was my closest friend on the team," he said. "We had a lot of talks and went through a lot of things together. I enjoyed every teammate I had at the university, but Peeler and I were that Batman and Robin combo."

******

The man from Detroit and the man from Shelbyville had far more in common than fans may realize.

"Coach Stewart and I had a great relationship," Smith said. "I have heard different things about players who didn't like his coaching style, but I thought he was an excellent coach as far as the things he wanted to accomplish on the basketball court. Because I came from a hard coach in high school, I did what you had to do, and I didn't have any problems with Coach Stewart. That's what I did—try to do the things he asked me to do. That's why my career went the way it did."

******

Loyalty means a lot to Smith, and he hopes fans remember him as a person who went about his game and his life the right way.

"I want to be remembered as a good guy, as a person who came to school and honored a four-year commitment to play at the university," he said, "I want to be remembered as a hard-nosed player who went out and did the things necessary to win.

"One of the other special things about playing at the University of Missouri is that I only lost three home games in my career. Fifty-nine and three is not bad."

Living the Border Battle

No one needed to explain the importance of the Kansas rivalry to Chris Heller when he became a Tiger. He literally grew up in the midst of it. Heller attended private Rockhurst High School in Kansas City on State Line Road, the street that divides Missouri from Kansas.

"We lived on the Missouri side for two years while I was in high school, then we moved over to the Kansas side for two years," he said. "I was splitting the line."

Heller was highly recruited after being named Mr. Basketball in Missouri his senior year. He visited Missouri, Kansas, Kansas State, UCLA and SMU.

"I narrowed it down to Kansas and Missouri," he said. "I wanted to stay close to home. Kansas and Missouri had good programs at that time and historically had been pretty good. I got to know Larry Brown pretty well before he left Kansas, then Roy Williams, and obviously, Coach Stewart. It was down to those two schools, and I knew either way I was going to do well. I had a sister at KU, so that made it interesting."

Heller chose the Tigers.

"From where I was from, it was a big in-house rivalry," he said. "We look back and laugh at it now, but at the time that I signed with Missouri, it was a month or so before my sister even spoke to me."

Heller immediately stepped into the middle of a rivalry that had significance not only in the Big Eight

Conference but nationally. The Tigers held the top spot in the nation for four weeks that season, and Kansas also was ranked No. 1.

"That was the 1989-90 season, when we were 1-2 in the nation, back and forth with Kansas," he said. "It was a great Mizzou team with four seniors, so there was a lot of experience. It was nice coming in as a freshman and being on the No. 1 team in the country.

"It was a big adjustment, though. In high school, I was always 'the guy.' The competition level became a lot, lot higher, and a lot of it is psychological. You come in thinking, 'I'm the man, and I'm going to play right away.' But in college, everybody was the man."

******

As it turns out, Heller's Tigers were evenly matched with the rival Jayhawks.

"It was a big rivalry," he said. "All through high school, I had gone to Larry Brown's camps, so I knew a lot of people over there. My freshman year, we beat them home and away. My sophomore and junior years, we lost all four games. Then my senior year, we won both games again. So I finished at .500 against Kansas."

******

Tiger basketball fans remember Heller's stellar play in the 1993 Big Eight Tournament in Kansas City. The Tigers were a 5-9 in conference play and entered the tournament as the seventh seed. But Heller and the Tigers got on a roll, beating Oklahoma State, Iowa State and Kansas State on the way to the postseason title.

"We as a team had struggled and went into the tournament down at the bottom of the league," he said.

"Nobody expected us to do anything. I personally had a good weekend, but everybody did. We came in there very loose, and we played very well. That was one of the more memorable things to me."

Heller also saw the highs and lows of NCAA Tournament competition. In his freshman year, the Tigers were shocked by Northern Iowa in the first round. But in his senior season, the Tigers made a run at their first Final Four before losing to Arizona in the Elite Eight in Los Angeles.

******

Heller's relationship with Stewart mirrored his play.

"We had a good relationship, but it was kind of up and down," he said. "I played well at the end of my sophomore and junior years but not so well at the start of my senior year. Our relationship went as my performance on the court went. But I have a lot of respect for Coach Stewart. He even wrote my letter of recommendation for law school."

Heller believes his playing days prepared him well for life in law school and beyond.

"You have so little time when you are playing basketball," he said. "You have to manage your time, or you fall behind. You know what needs to be done and how to get it done. When I was going through law school, I thought, 'This is the first time in my life that all I have to do is just to go to school.'"

Even the prodding from Stewart has paid dividends.

"I have to laugh when I see people on the job intimidated by the people above them in the company," he said. "I had Norm Stewart yell at me for five years [including a redshirt year because of injury]. I don't worry about it. There's nothing I haven't heard."

Heart of a Tiger

Brian Grawer has been around Mizzou basketball for longer than he can remember. His father, Rich Grawer, was head coach at DeSmet High School in St. Louis, an assistant under Norm Stewart at Missouri and head coach at St. Louis University.

"I cannot remember very much about living here in Columbia," Grawer said. "I lived here for eight months when I was probably three years old, so I can't remember much about it. But it was great to have relationships with superstars like Stipo and other guys who played here at Mizzou that my dad had connections with.

"I feel pretty privileged to be able to grow up in a basketball family. I think I grew up knowing and understanding more about the game than just an average player would be able to do, especially with Dad's experience and his relationship with Coach Stewart. I had a good idea of what I was getting into and what kind of coach he was when I decided to come play. Not only did I have a dad who coached with Coach Stewart but I had a dad who was a Division I coach. I wasn't naive when I came into the college ranks. I understood the struggles and how hard it was going to be for me to succeed."

Even with the Mizzou connections, however, it was not a slam dunk that Grawer would end up a Tiger.

"I knew you had to keep your options open," he said. "My dad did a great job of not steering me one way or the other. He left the whole deal up to me. I just knew when I came on campus on my visit that this would be a great place for me. Being able to play for your home state is something neat that not that many people can say they did in college."

******

How well did Rich Grawer prepare his son for college basketball?

"As a player in high school, I would come home after every game, and he would have a notebook written critiquing my play," Brian said. "It wasn't just during my game play; it also would have my stats from pregame warmups and from halftime warmups. He was just very detail-oriented, and he's just a great basketball mind. I know he was very in-depth with his scouting and very in-depth with how he prepared his team. He ran a lot of sets and was a very structured coach, similar to Coach Stewart.

"I didn't have the opportunity to play for my dad, but it was a privilege to go play for somebody that has so many wins as Coach Stewart has and who will one day be in the Hall of Fame."

******

Ask Grawer about team accomplishments from 1997 to 2001, and he will reply with one word: Kansas.

"Always, when you talk about Missouri basketball, your first memories have to be your games against KU," he said.

Quin Snyder
(AP/WWP)

"As a freshman, they were ranked third in the nation when they came into the Hearnes Center. Just the feeling when you played KU, when they came here, you knew you were going to beat them. You knew you had the advantage over them. I don't know how it occurred. They had Paul Pierce, Raef LaFrentz and Ryan Robertson, and being able to beat them was an unbelievable feeling. We had a lot of key wins that year."

Another of those victories that season came at home against national powerhouse Maryland.

"That was a big game, because the year before, Mizzou went to Maryland and lost by 30 or so," he said. "It was the first big-name team to come to the Hearnes Center that season. We had a big win [83-79], and that sparked us for the Big 12 season.

"Illinois was a special game as well. It was back in my hometown, and it gave an opportunity for my brothers and sisters around the country to come back to St. Louis around Christmas and watch me play once every year in person. It was a great game, no matter how good either team was. I have always said one team can be No. 1 in the nation and the other team can be winless, and you knew it was going to be a battle every game."

******

Grawer also had the opportunity to play under coach Quin Snyder. He ended his career in an exciting NCAA tournament game against Duke, the eventual national champion. The game also was the first matchup between Coach Q and Coach K.

"Losing to the national champs is a great way to go out," he said. "I played against Jason Williams, Shane Battier and Mike Dunleavey and all those guys. We gave them a heck of a run, and we knew Mizzou was on the way up again, and we had something to do with that."

******

Fans loved Grawer for doing the little things that don't always show up in the statistics. But anyone who thumbs through the school record books might be surprised at how many times his name turns up.

"When most people talk about my career there, they talk about my three-point shooting or my free throws," he said. "But I finished in second career list in steals [195], one behind Anthony Peeler. That is something I am very proud of, because when people think of Brian Grawer, they don't think of steals. To be up there with my name sandwiched between Anthony Peeler and Melvin Booker is something special.

"I am proud of setting the single-season record for free-throw percentage [.905] my junior year. I am in the top 10 categories of free-throw percentage, three-point percentage, three-pointers made and steals. When I came in, I did not believe that those things could be accomplished. I will always be in the history books, and that's something that not many people can say when they finish their careers here."

A dark day for Mizzou turned into a bright spot individually for Grawer.

"I always remember my senior year when we were at Iowa State," he said. "That's when Kareem Rush was injured and Clarence Gilbert was suspended. Coach Snyder started me and four freshmen, so it was kind of a difficult game. No one gave us any credit, and Iowa State was ranked in the top 10. I hit eight threes that game. It was a good moment for our team. Everybody likes the scoring. Everybody likes to remember those games. That's one of the memories I'll always take with me."

******

Grawer joined Snyder's staff as a student assistant for the 2002-2003 season. As a longtime student of the game and now a coach, how would he have scouted Brian Grawer?

"I'm not going to surprise you. I'm not going to do things that your jaw is going to drop on the floor and you're going to say, 'Man, did he just do that?' I'm not going to be like Ricky Paulding or Anthony Peeler and do amazingly athletic things. But when I'm away from the ball, you had better stay with me. You'd better not lose track of me, because I'll find the open spot. My teammates will find me, and I'll knock down a heart-breaking three. I'm going to be a very steady player who's going to get teammates involved and do little things to help my team win. I'm not going to blow by you, but if you give me an opportunity, I can. You have to respect me.

"You can't just look at the exterior and think you can walk all over me because I'm a five-foot-10 little scrawny guy. I'm able to do some things that people didn't exactly feel I could do when they played against me. But after I had already done it, they started to bear in on me. If you forget about me, then I'll hurt you. I did that and hit some key shots against big opponents at key times. I wasn't afraid to take a big shot. I wasn't scared to go to the free-throw line and knock in some free throws. I just did whatever Coach Stewart or Coach Snyder needed me to do."

******

Grawer has to pinch himself sometimes when he realizes he once again is wearing the black and gold.

"It's unbelievable just to be able to come back to where you played for four years and gave so much to the university and where the fans supported you so well," he said. "Missouri basketball is a special family, and once you leave, you're never forgotten. It's great to be back. I get chills sometimes on the sideline watching the guys playing."

******

Some players' reputations grow over time, while others quickly are forgotten. Grawer is gratified that fans have fond memories of him and his style of play.

"People remember me the right way, as a hard-nosed player who gave them everything he had, every time he stepped on the floor," he said. "I was a fan's player. They can relate to me, because I was smaller than a lot of fans. I was able to go out there and play against six-foot-eight, six-foot-nine guys and be successful. I dove on the floor whenever I could, I tried to be very energetic and lively and get the crowd involved. I'm very happy how people remember me as a player. They remember me as somebody who just gave them everything he could, every time he stepped on the floor."

2

Tales from
Missouri Football

Setting the Standard

Officially, the Missouri Tigers play their home games at Memorial Stadium in Columbia. But for fans throughout the Show Me State, it is known simply as Faurot Field.

As the years slip away, however, fewer people remember Don Faurot the man. John Kadlec, who has been a player, assistant coach or broadcaster at Mizzou since 1946, knows as well as anybody what Faurot meant to the university and its football program.

"He was a very, very tough coach on the field," Kadlec said. "He was fair, but he was tough. He knew what it took to play football, and that meant discipline. I'll tell you this about Coach Faurot: I've never known another coach in the country who knew as much about the game. He could coach offense or defense. Some coaches major in one side or the other, but this guy was so adept that he could coach every position. He knew the guard, the tackle, the end. Bob Broeg of the *St. Louis Post-Dispatch* said this, and I agree: 'He could take his 11 and beat you, then take your 11 and beat you.'

"He was a real student of the game. He coached defensive backs in the Blue-Gray game until he was about 85 years old. The head coaches down there were amazed at how contemporary he was on pass defense. He was a brilliant guy. He would go out and watch practice every day here at Missouri in his later years.

The last time I watched practice with him, he was 93, and about four weeks later, he passed away."

Faurot was a three-sport letterman for the Tigers from 1922 to 1924, then became head football coach from 1935 to 1956. During his tenure, the Tigers compiled a record of 101-79-10. He won the school's first Big Six title in 1939 and led it to its first bowl bid, the 1940 Orange Bowl against Georgia Tech.

******

Faurot's contributions to Mizzou are numerous. Perhaps his biggest contribution to the game of college football was the innovation of the Split-T formation in 1941. It still is being used more than 60 years later, and popular offenses such as the wishbone, wingbone and veer are based on Faurot's option play. The Tigers, of course, ran the formation to perfection.

"Our quarterback was Bus Entsminger," Kadlec said. "Bus was an outstanding quarterback off the Split-T. He could do things off that Split-T that no one else in the country could do until Darrell Royal and Jack Mitchell at Oklahoma. Entsminger was the first great original Split-T quarterback."

******

Kadlec, who played guard on offense and tackle and guard on defense, said the Faurot offense could be unstoppable when it was firing on all cylinders.

"There was a guy from Kansas City named John Glorioso who was a terrific halfback," he said. "The other halfback was named Dick Braznell, out of University City, Missouri He was a left-handed passer and played right halfback. When we pitched him the ball on a left sweep, he had a great arm. I think as a halfback, he threw more touchdown passes than anyone ever at Missouri. He was really good. Our fullback was Win Carter, who went into the FBI and became a top executive at Ford Motor Co."

******

Faurot continued as director of athletics until 1967, hiring such outstanding coaches as John "Hi" Simmons in baseball and Frank Broyles and Dan Devine in football. In 1972, the university named the playing surface Faurot Field in his honor, which was only fitting, because he once helped sod the field as a graduate student in agriculture in 1926.

******

Kadlec came to Mizzou from Southside Catholic High School in St. Louis for one simple reason. "I never had an opportunity to go to another school," he said. "Missouri was the only one that ever wanted me."

However, the hard-nosed lineman earned the respect of his coach.

"Coach Faurot selected me on his all-time both-way team," he said. "I was very fortunate he did that."

******

Faurot thought enough of Kadlec to hire him as a graduate assistant in 1951, then as a full-time assistant in 1952.

"Of course, he scheduled all the big, tough games," Kadlec said. "We would open with Ohio State, then play SMU when the great Doak Walker was there. I was fortunate to work for four great coaches—Don Faurot, Frank Broyles, Dan Devine and Al Onofrio. I was very lucky and had some great experiences with these coaches and the great players we recruited."

******

The name Frank Broyles is as synonymous with the University of Arkansas as Don Faurot or Dan Devine is with Missouri. People often forget that he coached the Tigers in the 1957 season, compiling a record of 5-4-1.

"We only had him here nine months," Kadlec said. "Frank Broyles was a terrific coach. A lot of people held it against him because he left Missouri, but he felt he had an opportunity at Arkansas. At that time, Arkansas was a little more football-oriented than Missouri, for some reason. They were putting more money into it, and he got a tremendous salary down there."

******

Kadlec worked under four coaches—Don Faurot, Frank Broyles, Dan Devine and Al Onofrio—who would be a good start for a coaching Hall of Fame. What were the similarities and differences?

"Dan Devine was a great manager," Kadlec said. "He could manage the players, and he could manage his staff. That meant he was a great organization guy. That was his strong suit.

"Faurot's strong suit was football, football, football. Broyles's strong suit was football, football and organization. Onofrio knew the game as well as anybody and was a great, great defensive coach. He was a terrific recruiter.

"I don't know any team that has had all the pro prospects we recruited off of one team, guys like James Wilder, Johnnie Poe, Eric Wright, Kurt Peterson, Howard Richards and Jerome Sally. All those guys went to the pros. That's a hell of a lot off one team. Coach Onofrio was a terrific coach and an excellent recruiter in home with the parents.

"I've been very fortunate, because I've learned so much from those four coaches."

******

Don Faurot and Dan Devine head the list of the 30 men who have served as head coaches of the Tigers. Almost as impressive is the list of Tiger assistants who went on to distinguished careers as head coaches at major colleges or in the NFL. They include Phil

Bengston (Green Bay Packers), Jerry Claiborne (Virginia Tech, Maryland and Kentucky), Jim Donnan (Georgia), Dirk Koetter (Arizona State), Vince Tobin (Arizona Cardinals and Detroit Lions) and Andy Reid (Philadelphia Eagles).

******

Kadlec has participated in some of the most memorable games in Mizzou history.

"As a player, I never lost to Kansas, and that probably is the biggest accomplishment," he said. "In those days, the KU rivalry was a terrific, high-pitched rivalry. As a coach, I think of several victories. Beating Notre Dame at South Bend, 30-26, and beating Alabama on *Monday Night Football* were two of the greatest victories.

"Then we had some great victories against Nebraska with Coach Onofrio's team. I remember one in particular when we were losing in the fourth quarter, 10-0. We were playing in Lincoln, and they were ranked No. 12 in the nation. In the fourth quarter, we scored 21 points and beat them, 21-10. That was in 1974. The Alabama game, the Notre Dame game and the 22-21, last-second victory at Ohio State, were among my most memorable games as a coach."

******

Al Onofrio became legendary for upsetting several major teams during the 1970s. However, those killer schedules may have taken their toll later in the season, Kadlec said.

"In 1976, we played at USC, at Illinois and at Ohio State," he said. "Now, when you play three teams like that, you have a hell of a chance of getting kids hurt. By the time the conference rolled around, we were kind of beaten up. That's why I like what's going on now in college football, playing easier nonconference schedules early in the season."

******

When Kadlec coached, there wasn't the alphabet soup of bowl games that there is today. It was much harder to qualify for postseason play, and Devine's team even voted down the opportunity to play in several bowls because of their lackluster records.

"I can remember back in the 1960s, we had 7-3 records and would be staying home," he said. "Missouri may have gone to 10 more bowls under today's selection process."

Linebacker Andy Russell remembers one of Devine's early teams turning down a bid.

"In 1961, we came in second in conference, got invited to the Bluebonnet Bowl, and Coach Devine made the mistake of asking us to vote whether we wanted to play," he said.

"We voted it down, which really shocked Devine. My senior year, 1962, we came in second to Oklahoma, and we did go play a good Georgia Tech team in the Bluebonnet Bowl and beat them."

Devine learned a lesson about letting players vote, said offensive lineman Francis Peay.

"The seniors had voted down the Gator Bowl in my junior year," he said. "The next year, Coach Devine said, 'There will be no vote.'"

Devine Intervention

How do you replace Don Faurot and Frank Broyles? With Dan Devine, who became one of most beloved men in Missouri as head coach from 1958 to 1970. It would be hard to find a former player who doesn't treasure his memories of Devine.

Francis Peay, an All-America offense tackle in 1965, may know Devine as well as anyone. Peay later played professionally under Devine with the Green Bay Packers and served on Devine's coaching staff at the University of Notre Dame.

"I probably had one of the more unique relationships with Coach Devine," he said. "I was in his doghouse for awhile. They wanted to make a tight end out of me. I came in from junior college and didn't have spring practice, and they are going to make this tight end out of me. I couldn't catch the ball. I wasn't particularly happy realizing I had only two seasons and was wasting one. Johnny Roland was kind of my counselor, and I said, 'John, why would they not move me back to tackle, which is where they recruited me?'"

Teammate Conrad Hitchler remembers the story somewhat differently: "Francis Peay was going to kill Devine."

Devine finally started Peay at tackle in the next-to-last game of his junior season, and he became a fixture at the position.

"Coach Devine made that possible, and I appreciated and respected the fact," Peay said. "Mr. Devine made a statement during my senior year. He said to the team, 'Do you have any idea who the best player on this team is?' I figured he was going to say Johnny Roland. But he said, 'Francis Peay—he never makes a mistake.' That was his way of bringing me back into the fold with the football team."

******

By contrast, running back Norris Stevenson never got close to Devine until after his playing days.

"It's a two-stage relationship," Stevenson said. "While I was at Missouri, it was coach-athlete, and it really never got much further than that. We really developed the relationship we had in the time after. I got to know him from the standpoint that we took the time to know each other.

"It was over those years that we had the chance to sit down and talk. Very often, when he would come to St. Louis, he'd give me a ring, and we'd meet for lunch. There was a very close relationship that developed as a result. He was able to talk with me about some of the things that had happened. He was a very sensitive person in the first place, and he became even more so to the extent that he wanted to understand what went on."

******

Andy Russell remembers Devine as a superb recruiter when he was a highly touted high school player in Ladue, Missouri.

"Coach Devine had the mayor of St. Louis call my parents, and he had the governor call my parents," he said. "He knew how to do it. He had all of the big businessmen in St. Louis promise me a bright future. Nothing illegal, but they made you feel if you left the state, you were some kind of bad person.

"He had my parents go to Columbia without me. They sold my mother, because they took her into the library and showed her around and convinced her they had a fine academic institution as well as a good sports program.

"Devine really put together a team of outstanding young men. There were no petty jealousies. He preached teamwork, and the chemistry was absolutely perfect. I am so glad I went there; it worked out beautifully. I was fortunate to have had that opportunity to play for such a great coach and a great staff."

******

Roger Wehrli, an All-America defensive back, was hardly recruited at all. But like Russell, he loved playing for Devine.

"He was a wonderful coach," Wehrli said. "My two favorite coaches were Dan Devine and Don Coryell of the St. Louis Cardinals. They couldn't be two more opposites. Still, you had great respect for both of them. Coach Devine was a great motivator who got the most out of the players and the talent he had. He left most of the individual technique coaching up to the individual coaches. But he was a master at taking the team and getting it ready to play by Saturday."

When Wehrli arrived on campus, John Kadlec quickly learned the futility of arguing with Devine.

"I was on the offensive staff at that time, and we thought that when we recruited Wehrli that we were going to get him on offense," he said. "In the very first meeting, coach Devine put Roger's tag on the personnel board on the defensive side, and boy, we started arguing. Coach Devine said, 'That's the end of it. Roger is playing defense. We need speed on defense.'"

Devine's players have long tried to figure out what made their coach tick, and Hitchler believes he may have come as close as anyone.

"One time, I said, 'Coach, it appears you have three different philosophies about how you interact with players,'" he said. "'One player, you kick in the ass and scream and holler at him. One player, you pat on the ass and say what a great job he is doing. And another player, you just leave alone.' I was one he just left alone. He recognized the different personalties in players and treated them differently. Whatever it was, he was trying to get the most out of all of his players.

"Coach Devine was a unique person. There were a lot of players at the time who would say, 'I hate that guy.' But if he walked by on campus and say 'hi,' you could see immediately that those guys would straighten up: 'Gee, the coach spoke to me.'

"Coach Devine was not worried about being liked by the players, but he was concerned with being respected. Too many coaches today—and thank God we have one now who doesn't—have wanted to be liked by their players. It's not necessary."

Breaking the Barrier

Dan Devine left an incredible legacy on the field, one that the program has spent decades trying to replicate. But perhaps his greatest legacy to the university was successfully integrating the team by respecting all of his players, black or white. Devine saw not color, but talent.

Frank Broyles had recruited Norris Stevenson from St. Louis in 1957 as the program's first African-American player. He remembers those turbulent times.

"This was before the start of civil rights," he said. "There were smatterings and indications that things were changing. Martin Luther King was a pretty young guy, and I think the name was vaguely familiar to me. My last year of high school began the integration of public schools. There are things we wanted to accomplish, and we assumed the only way we could do it was by going to a college that was primarily white.

"Frankly, it was something you were led to believe. I did want to get an education, and that was as important to me as football, because I had been raised that way. The experience at Missouri wasn't totally unexpected. It was very disappointing when people you were close to would literally turn on you. I think there are many things we are meant to carry, and to some extent, they did happen. On the other hand, I kind of wonder if it had to happen. There are things that happened to me that I haven't been able to let go."

In many ways, the adjustment was more difficult academically and socially than athletically.

"It was very different, adjusting to a primarily white school," Stevenson said. "Again, having to learn to adjust to that, the classroom situation. The college life itself is more than football. It's a social experience. It was not unexpected, because it was the nature of the times. Most of us came thinking we were going to have some difficulties. I wanted to play football. I wasn't aware of breaking any barriers, other than the fact that there were not a lot of blacks at the university. I thought I could play there."

******

Devine arrived a year later and helped smooth the transition. "Coach Devine came my sophomore year," Stevenson said. "He was a guy who walked in and seemed to be in such control. It was an enjoyable experience."

John Kadlec was a young assistant on that coaching staff.

"We treated everybody the same," he said. "I recruited Norris Stevenson, and Norris and I have talked about this. I didn't say, 'We want you to come here, you will be the first black player.' He said, 'Coach, you never mentioned that situation while you were recruiting me.' I didn't, because I recruited Norris as a student athlete, as a football player. I didn't care if he was black or white. That was the theme of all of our teams under Devine and Al Onofrio. We treated everybody the same. Dan had a great touch will all those kids."

******

Al Onofrio, an assistant coach in those years, also credits Devine for his even-handed approach.

"That was very important to him and his staff," he said. "There wasn't any problem at all that way. He worked at it and made all of the players feel they were a part of the team and that everything would be based upon how well they played. We were fortunate that we didn't have the problems that other schools had, and it was mainly from the philosophy that Dan Devine had. Dan was the one who set the policy."

******

That approach is what convinced running back Johnny Roland to come to Missouri as a top prospect from Corpus Christi, Texas.

"I was pretty highly recruited out of Roy Miller High School," he said. "I was sought after by Oklahoma, Nebraska, the University of California, the University of Arizona, Illinois and Indiana.

"At that time, the Southwest Conference was not recruiting minority athletes. If I was going to play major college football, I was going to have to leave the state of Texas. I signed up with Oklahoma initially, but upon reconsideration, I ended up at Missouri. The Midwest people were just so warm and friendly, and I liked the black and gold uniform. It was the camaraderie of the coaches and the players that I would be there at least two years with, and in some cases three. They were young, hungry and wanted to go places."

Although Stevenson didn't realize it at the time, he was influential in attracting Roland to Mizzou.

"Norris Stevenson was a big influence on me going there," Roland said. "When I was being recruited in those days, you used to be able to go to the movies and see the highlights of the week. One particular Saturday, I was at a movie and saw Norris and Mel West score touchdowns against Oklahoma, and that pretty much swung me toward going to Missouri."

Roland, like Stevenson, believes Devine cared about him only as a person and as a football player.

"He was colorblind," he said. "If you produced and performed for him on the football field, you were his guy. He was my mentor, he was the one who offered me a job. I took it and have been coaching ever since. In those days, I didn't think I would ever want to be a coach. He kept telling me, 'When you get done playing that silly little kid's game, I've got a job for you.' Finally, I took him up on it after the 1973 season when I knew I was done as a player."

******

The story continues, because friends of Roland's helped steer Francis Peay to Missouri. Although the two had their disagreements when Devine tried to convert him to tight end, Peay appreciates his even-handed approach to race relations.

"During my junior year, Gayle Sayers had been arrested at a demonstration." he said. "Coach Devine spoke to us and said that it is impossible for us not to have our players involved in demonstrations and that we were one family and one team. It was kind of like a father's advice: 'We will fight the battles that need to be fought in this regard for you.'

"As a result, everywhere we traveled, we went first class. We went to the Sugar Bowl in New Orleans. The old American Football League had held its All-Star game there the year before, and the black players had pulled out. Now we are going to New Orleans. Coach Devine said, 'We will all stay together as one team. You will not have to enter by a separate entrance.'

"Coach Devine had more black players than any-body else in the Big Eight conference. When you stop and think about it, I would have to say that man was connected politically, because he was able to do some things. Nothing from the outside affected us. I think he was always very sensitive about our relationship, and I always said, 'Coach, everything is OK.'"

Triple Threat from the '30s

What can be more impressive than lettering in three sports in college? How about winning a conference championship in each sport?

"I was born in Kentucky but went to high school in Columbia," Clay Cooper said. "I was a three-sport guy—football, basketball and track—and I was fortunate to be on teams that won Big Six championships in all three sports."

Cooper arrived on campus in 1936 to play wingback and defensive halfback for coach Don Faurot.

"The substitution rules were a little different in those days," he said. "If you played in one quarter and came out of the game, you couldn't go back in until the next quarter. So we played both ways."

Cooper was part of some memorable games.

"In 1939, my senior year, we played Georgia Tech in the Orange Bowl," he said. "We beat Nebraska pretty bad that season [27-13], and we beat Oklahoma at home, 7-6. We had a crowd of 39,000 or 40,000, which was a sellout, because that was before the stadium was added onto."

The coaching staff encouraged football players to run track in the spring.

"In those days, nobody had weight programs, so you played another sport," Cooper said. "I ran the quarter-mile. I was not a great track man, but I ran in a relay of four guys running a quarter-mile each. I remember running on that mile relay team at Nebraska to win the Big Six title."

Finally, he was part of the 1938-39 basketball team that went 12-6 and won the conference championship. "I was fortunate to play," he said. "I was a sort of a forward and wing guy. We didn't have point guards like they do today, but that is really the position I played."

******

Cooper joined Faurot's staff in 1947 and began a distinguished coaching career.

"Don Faurot could outwork most people," he said. "He had a tremendous energy. He was a great offensive coach, but he didn't like to fool with defense. When he was finishing up his career, you had coaches like Bear Bryant and Bud Wilkinson who stressed both defense and offense, and that hurt Don a little."

Cooper coached defensive backs for most of his career, including All-Americas such as Roger Wehrli and John Moseley. As recruiting coordinator for many of those years, he steered top talent toward the defensive side of the line.

"I was able to recruit some good football players and sort of hide them out so nobody would know where they were, then put them on defense," he said.

******

Cooper has nothing but fond memories of his many years as a player and coach at Missouri.

"Working with the players I had was fun for me, because they had talent and responded so well to whatever we told them to do," he said. "Every year, I thought we could win the championship and go undefeated. You had the anticipation that you could beat anybody. We had people with great character who had talent, and as a consequence, we won a lot of games and had fun.

"I played at Missouri in the 1930s and coached in the '40s, '50s, '60s, '70s and '80s. That's pretty good."

Building a Winner

Despite the race barriers at many universities, Norris Stevenson had a number of options when looking for a place to play his college football, particularly in the Big Ten conference.

"I had visited the University of Indiana and had been offered by the University of Wisconsin," he said. "I also had been offered by Minnesota. I never figured out exactly what led me to Missouri, but I connected with the coaches. At the time, it was Frank Broyles and his staff."

But before long, it was Dan Devine and his staff.

"I didn't think they were the same kind of coach at all," Stevenson said. "Both of them were outstanding coaches—that goes without saying. Both were disciplinarians, as any coach generally is. But beyond that, the style of play was different. I though Coach Broyles was much more offensively minded. Coach Devine came in and maybe saw our limitations as a team offensively and just went to a defensive set. He used what he had."

As it turns out, Stevenson, a Tiger from 1958 until 1960, was on the ground floor of the best decade in Missouri football history.

"It was the beginning of the Devine era, all the winning seasons," he said. "But it seems we were so busy defeating ourselves that first year. By the time we were seniors, things were beginning to come together.

In many ways, it surprised most of us in terms of how much of a team we had become in those three years."

******

Stevenson's senior year, 1960, encompassed perhaps the greatest high and greatest low in Mizzou history. The Tigers had a national championship in their grasp after upsetting Oklahoma in Norman, only to have it slip away by losing to archrival Kansas at home in the season finale.

"Of course, my last year was the almost-miracle," he said. "That is in my memory, along with the guys who were on that team. It was a really fine football team. It wasn't a team necessarily with any great individuals, but a lot of very good football players. Coach could pretty much run the backfield in interchangeably. We were pretty quick, and that helped out.

"People almost always are asking me to say something about Oklahoma. That spoke for itself—it was a big game for me. But I've often gone back to something else, a game against Penn State out there earlier. It wasn't so much that it was the best game, but it was a game you felt you were beginning to establish your own confidence as a player. They were as well known then as they are now. That was really a big one for most of us, because we had gone to the East Coast and beaten the best."

Missouri won that game in State College, Pennsylvania, 21-8.

******

Much has been made of Stevenson's courage in breaking the color barrier at Missouri. He gives much of the credit to the support of his teammates.

"There were some guys I value tremendously, guys such as Jim Miles, Dan Larose and Ron Taylor," he said.

"I hate to do this, because I will forget somebody. Sometimes, it was harder for them than for us as far as the racial atmosphere. If it weren't for some of those guys, I don't know if I would have stayed."

******

Stevenson hopes that his example made the way easier for the student athletes who came after him.

"I would like to be remembered as the guy who got there first and did the best he could," he said. "I just wanted to get an education. I enjoyed playing football, I really enjoyed it. When I got on the football field, I could be somebody else. There were things I could accomplish. I wasn't the guy they thought I was, and maybe I changed some minds for the better. Maybe some people ran into an African-American player later and remember that we were all just trying to make it."

Hard-Hitting Defensive Leadership

Missouri football history is filled with small-town kids who always wanted to play at the state university and big-city kids who overcame the odds to realize their dreams. Linebacker Andy Russell was neither, but the son of a top Monsanto Company executive who grew up in Detroit, Chicago, Westchester County, N.Y., and the St. Louis suburb of Ladue.

In some ways, he may have been the unlikeliest of football heroes.

"My parents weren't into sports," he said. "My dad came over on the boat from Scotland and wanted me to work right away."

Russell, an avid mountain climber today, initially had the Colorado Buffaloes at the top of his list of colleges.

"I love the state," he said. "But they had offered me some things they probably shouldn't have, so my father said, 'You're not going there.' It was good advice, because my senior year, most of the seniors at Colorado were not allowed to play."

******

Russell is best remembered as an outstanding linebacker for Mizzou and later the Pittsburgh Steelers. But like many players under Dan Devine, he played both ways in college.

"I led the team in rushing in 1962 as a fullback, which is unusual for a linebacker," he said. "In fact, I was recruited to be a running back. I was a much better offensive than defensive player in high school. I remember my high school coach telling me, 'You'd better get tough on defense, because Devine likes defensive players.'

"I ended up starting my sophomore year as a linebacker, not as a fullback. Devine would flank me out. I had pretty good hands in those days, and on long yardage, he would make the fullback a flanker, which was pretty unusual. That was fun for me to do that. On critical third-down, move-the-sticks kinds of times, he would occasionally throw the ball. He hated to throw the ball. He wanted to run the ball every down if he could. Throwing the ball on first down was not an option.

"I'm not sure, but I think I led the nation in interceptions. I had a lot of interceptions."

******

Russell remembers the early 1960s as a golden era for Tiger football.

"I think it was spectacular," he said. "It was just a great thrill to be on that ride. In my freshman year, 1959, Missouri went to the Orange Bowl and lost to a good Fran Tarkenton Georgia team. My sophomore year, we were ranked in the top 20 starting out, so we knew we were pretty good, but no one expected us to move up the way we did. We went to the Snake Pit in Oklahoma and beat a very good Bud Wilkinson-coached Oklahoma team decisively with one game to go, putting us No. 1 in the nation. In those days, they picked the No. 1 team in the country before the bowl games. So we were that close to a ring in 1960.

"We had to play the final game against KU at Mizzou, and KU had not had a particularly good year. They had some good players, but they came in and upset us. I remember being shocked by that, because I thought we were a much better team. I was only a sophomore, but I was starting at linebacker. We had the home field, everything, but Kansas took that ring away from us. I saw John Hadl in the pros and kidded him about that. We played Navy in the Orange Bowl."

Russell's teammate, lineman Conrad Hitchler, said Devine took full responsibility for the loss that knocked Mizzou out of a national championship.

"He said he let too many distractions come in and it was his fault, that he ran us too much that week after a long season," Hitchler said. "We would have been No. 1. We went on to beat Navy in a bowl game, and everyone ranked ahead of us got beaten."

******

That 1960 Orange Bowl, which Missouri won 21-14, was a highlight of Russell's career.

"That was a big thrill," he said. "The president of

the United States was up in the stands rooting for Navy. They had the Heisman Trophy winner, Joe Bellino, but we shut him down. That was the highlight, which happened my sophomore year. I also loved playing in the Bluebonnet Bowl against Georgia Tech. We routed Oklahoma in 1960 in the Snake Pit, and it was a big thrill."

It was in those years that Missouri took its place among the Big Eight's elite teams.

"Kansas was the big rival, but Oklahoma was consistently the best team we played," Russell said. "Nebraska was just starting to come on. We beat them all three years, but we could see them getting better. They brought in a bunch of 22-year-old marines. They were getting really serious."

******

Russell would not like to have been an offensive coordinator scheming a game plan against the Missouri defense.

"Opposing coaches when they set up to play a Mizzou defense knew they were in for a workout," he said. "Devine preached defense. We always prided ourselves in being one of the top defensive teams against the rush.

"I remember one time, somebody scored standing up against us. Coach Devine showed us a film and said, 'Nobody has scored against us standing up in a year and a half.' He went crazy. He showed us this film of somebody going across the goal line standing up, and it drove him crazy. I've never heard of anything like that."

The defense turned it up a notch against high-caliber competition.

"We held Gayle Sayers to 73 yards," Russell said. "Joe Bellino, the shifty halfback at Navy, was the Heisman winner, and they said at the Orange Bowl he cannot be tackled in the open field by one player. Devine just went crazy. We smoked him. He had minus-two yards rushing. The Heisman Trophy winner was blanked.

"Other coaches would say about us, 'These guys are well coached, they are not going to be where you want them to be, they are going to move into the holes.'"

******

When Russell played his final game for the Tigers, he was certain his football days were over.

"I did not expect to play professional football at all," he said. "My father had made me promise I would not play pro football. He was embarrassed to have a son so frivolous as to play a game for a living. Can you imagine?"

In those days, there were only 12 teams in the National Football League, so roster positions were few and far between. Even so, 11 of the teams sent Russell a standard query form for prospective players.

"The first question was, 'Are you interested in playing pro football?'" he said. "I wrote no and sent it back. I didn't even fill out the form. I had an ROTC commitment with two years of active service in Germany. I didn't think there was any way I could play pro football."

By this time, Russell's father was working in Europe for Monsanto, so he stayed on campus for the holidays. The NFL draft was held in December, before the bowl games.

"I went to work out, and some guy said, 'Hey, Russell, congratulations.' I said, 'Why?' He said, 'You were drafted.' I said, 'I can't be drafted'—I'm in the ROTC.' I thought he mean the military draft. I found out that some team called the Pittsburgh Steelers had drafted me in the 16th round. I told them on the phone they had wasted their draft pick. They said they would give me a signing bonus, let me do my military service and then resume my career.

"I started my rookie year and made the All-Rookie team. I loved it."

******

Despite all he has accomplished in life, few things rank higher than his Mizzou experience for Russell.

"I hope people remember me as a young man who totally appreciated the experience playing for such an outstanding university and such a great coaching staff," he said. "You talk about wonderful mentors to teach you the old-school values to go forward in life, I just feel blessed I had that opportunity. I was not as good of a college football player as I would have liked to have been, but I was able to achieve some of those goals in the pros. I was very proud to be captain of the team in 1962. I just loved the experience."

An All-America Career

Missouri fans will always be upset with Kansas for preventing the Tigers from winning the national championship in 1960. But on the other hand, a Kansas student helped nudge a future All-America lineman toward attending Mizzou.

Conrad Hitchler took a roundabout way from Paseo High School in Kansas City to Columbia.

"I played two years of high school football, then quit high school and went to the Marine Corps," he said. "I ended up playing service ball with some of the top players in the country, guys like Ron Beegle and Jim Mora. One of the guys went to Utah State. He said, 'You ought to consider going to Utah State,' and I had a scholarship to go there when I got out of the Marines. But I also had offers from Southern California and a couple of schools back on the East Coast.

"I got out in January and came back to Kansas City. I visited Missouri first and then KU. KU was mainly responsible for me going to Missouri. They fixed me up with this girl, and we were at a keg party down on the Kansas River. She said, 'Where else are you thinking about going?' and I said, 'Utah State, Southern California and Missouri.' She said, 'Missouri? All they do there is party and drink.'

"It was like a light bulb went on in my head. I had

kind of made up my mind that was where I was going anyway, but that was frosting on the cake."

******

Like many players on his team, his best memory is of beating Oklahoma to gain the No. 1 ranking in the nation.

"When we got back in Columbia, the fire trucks were there to meet us at the airport," he said. "They took the players through town on a fire truck with the sirens going. I don't know how many people were out there to meet us—probably fewer than what I imagine now. But there were a lot of people there. Then we went to the student union and everybody said something. The following week we got beaten by KU."

******

Winters in Columbia can get a little long, even for Missouri natives. One winter in particularly nearly cost the Tigers a star player.

"The second semester started, and it was snowing," Hitchler said. "I was sitting in class, thinking, 'Southern California.' I called Southern California, and they said, 'Come on. You'll probably have to go through El Toro Junior College, but we'll work everything out. We'll send you a plane ticket.' I was at the airport when they caught me."

******

It's hard to imagine any player enjoying a better month than Hitchler had to wrap up his senior season.

"I think Bill Callahan, the sports information director, called and told me I was going to be named to the All-America team," he said. "Then I heard it from one of the football writers at *Look* magazine.

"I got invited to go to New York for all those festivities. It was great month, that month of December. I went to New York, got back, practiced for a week, went to Houston for the Bluebonnet Bowl, got the lineman of the game award, got my nose broken and they operated on it that night. I got on a plane the next day and went to San Francisco to play in the East-West Shrine game, left there and went to Honolulu to play in the Hula Bowl game. You talk about being catered to and pampered—everything was taken care of. That's a month that can never be repeated."

Two-Way Success

Johnny Roland may well have been the biggest recruiting coup ever for Dan Devine at Missouri. Playing both ways, he figured in many of the team's biggest victories from 1962 to 1965.

Roland was the team's leading rusher as a sophomore, with 830 yards and 78 points. He was named All-America at defensive back after the 1965 season, although he continued to carry the ball. He even returned punts. Among his many honors is being named NFL Rookie of the Year for the St. Louis Cardinals and having his #23 jersey retired at Mizzou.

There has never been a player who arrived or left with such fanfare.

"My first game as a Tiger, I scored three touchdowns against the University of California-Berkeley," he said, "and I closed out my career by scoring three touchdowns against the University of Kansas."

******

Bob Broeg, Hall of Fame sportswriter for the *St. Louis Post-Dispatch*, has forgotten more about Mizzou football than most people ever knew. In his opinion, "The best all-around player on offense and defense was Johnny Roland."

******

Roland is a longtime assistant with the NFL's Arizona Cardinals. How would he have scouted Johnny Roland as a Tiger?

"A guy who played 60 minutes, because in those days, they had limited substitutions," he said. "I was on the field quite a bit as a punt returner, kickoff returner, offense and defense. If you were to scout me, you would have to say he is never off the field. When he was on the field, he was giving 100 percent and being a team player."

******

Roland's teams had a number of impressive victories against national powers.

"We beat Nebraska once," he said. "Oklahoma at that time was down a little bit, and we beat them a couple of times. We had some significant victories in the border war with Kansas, and we beat Minnesota a couple of times."

His team beat Georgia Tech 14-10 in the 1962 Bluebonnet Bowl, then beat a Florida team led by Steve Spurrier 20-18 in the 1966 Sugar Bowl. In that game, Roland threw an 11-yard touchdown pass to Earl Denny on a halfback option play.

******

As Roland works with young players today, he encourages them to respect the game as much as he did.

"I've always been a guy who loved to practice, loved the camaraderie in the locker room and loved to compete on the football field," he said. "The blessing for me was just being able to put on a uniform and go out there and perform and try to win ballgames. We were unknown, but we knew how good we were. We were strapping it on and coming at you. I gave my all, and I always took pride in being a professional about my job and left it out on the field."

Realizing a Dream

Some kids grow up dreaming of playing at Mizzou, while others have to be recruited heavily. Few players ever put as much effort into achieving their dream as Francis Peay, who became an All-America offensive tackle.

"It was a long, long road," he said. "I grew up right in the shadow of the University of Pittsburgh. I grew up in a housing project a five-minute walk from their stadium and practice field. My grade school and high school actually are on their campus. That's where my dream was born. I spent a lot of time at their practices, from about second grade on, and got put out a lot of times. Over the years, the coaching staff kind of got used to me.

"The University of Pittsburgh had not had many black players for whatever reason. For the most part, other than Syracuse, most of the eastern schools didn't have many black players. Black players in Pennsylvania were going west."

That's what Peay did, signing with the University of Arizona. It didn't take him long to regret his decision.

"I didn't feel it was going to fulfill my dream, which was playing in a bowl game," he said. "I wanted to be an All-America and decided to leave. I went to Cameron Junior College in Oklahoma."

His ultimate goal, however, was getting to Columbia.

"Johnny Roland had two high school buddies a year ahead of me at Arizona," he said. "They had spoken to me about Missouri and said Johnny really loved it. I had an early contact with Missouri, watching the *Ed Sullivan Show* and seeing Danny Larose as an All-American. Arizona played Missouri my freshman year, and Missouri won 17 to 7. Johnny scored a touchdown."

Even so, Peay committed to Oklahoma after a year at Cameron.

"I was all set to go to Oklahoma," he said. "Oklahoma was going to open up at the University of Pittsburgh the next season. Oklahoma had me, I was going to be a Sooner. But a sportswriter in Lawton, Oklahoma, said, 'Where do you really want to go to school, Oklahoma?' I said, 'No, the University of Missouri.' He printed it, and a Missouri alum living in Lawton, Oklahoma, called Coach Devine. I signed with Missouri sight unseen. It was a gut feeling, but I have never been quite so lucky."

******

Peay moved into a starting position late in his junior season and became an All-American as a senior. He only wishes he had been able to spend more time as a Tiger.

"Something I have always reflected upon is that I wish I would have had four years at Missouri," he said. "I think about the relationships that are developed over four years, coming in as freshmen together. In the two years I had, the Sugar Bowl was the highlight. I will never forget when each senior was called off the field individually, taking my helmet off and leaving the field in New Orleans. That was a thrill. But the gift that keeps on giving is the relationship with guys like Johnny Roland.

"I wish I could be remembered as a four-year Tiger in the same vein as Johnny Roland, Carl Reese and some of those guys I thought so much of. But in truth, Missouri was just a great experience in my life. I was fortunate I was able to realize my dreams. I want people to realize I will always be a Tiger."

******

After retiring from professional football, Peay coached a high school team in University City, Missouri.

"I got a call from Coach Devine asking me to join his staff at Notre Dame," he said. "I already had accepted a job at Wake Forest and was about ready to leave. But I couldn't turn down Coach Devine. I took the same flight to Chicago that I would have taken into Winston-Salem, but I went to South Bend instead."

From Small Town to the Big Time

Roger Wehrli was a high school legend in football, basketball and track in Northwest Missouri. But playing at small King City High School, he had few illusions of landing a scholarship to play at a Division I program.

"Being from such a small school, we weren't really scouted," he said. "In fact, as far as Missouri goes, I wasn't scouted at all in football. They did send the freshman basketball coach down our senior year to watch one of our basketball games, thinking they might be interested in me in basketball. But after I took my football pads off after my final high school game, I thought it would be the last time I put those on.

"I was recruited by Northwest Missouri State, William Jewell College and some of the other smaller colleges in Northwest Missouri. If I hadn't gotten the scholarship to Missouri, I probably would have gone to Maryville and played basketball."

Fortunately for both Wehrli and the Tigers, things turned out differently.

"My dad had known Sparky Stalcup and sent some films down to him," Wehrli said. "What did it is that I went to the state track meet, and coach Cooper, the defensive backfield coach, had come out to watch the athletes. I won the high hurdles, low hurdles and long jump and finished in the medals in the 220-yard dash.

"The story is—I guess it's true—is that they still had one scholarship they hadn't decided upon. From my performance in track, I showed I was a good all-around athlete, so they offered me that last scholarship. That was the only major college scholarship I had been offered."

That story certainly was true, according to assistant coach John Kadlec.

"We gave him the last scholarship," he said. "John Staggers from Jefferson City, who was a great player for us on our 1969 championship team, also received the last scholarship. Many times those tail-end scholarship kids turn out to be the best kids."

It didn't take long for Wehrli to realize he could compete on the highest level, although it required some adjustments.

"I felt like I could perform," he said. "The thing that was different was going from a really small town to a large campus and being by myself. The one thing players from places like Jeff City had that I didn't was using a lot of the same practice drills and techniques that Mizzou had. I'm sure their coaches went to clinics and things like that. So just the drills, fundamentals, techniques and things like that, a lot of the other players had a lot more knowledge of than I did, learning from scratch. It was quite a change. I have always said going from high school to college was a bigger change for me than going from Missouri to the pros."

******

Wehrli, unknown to him, was the subject of a fierce tug-of-war between offensive and defensive coaches.

"Even going into my freshman year, I didn't know until after a couple weeks of practice that they had me as a defensive player instead of an offensive player," he said. "We all were going through the same drills during two-a-days. When we went into spring ball my freshman year, there were several of us working out at defensive back. They moved one to wide receiver and put me in at defensive back. I can't remember if I knew for sure I was in the starting lineup in spring ball, because you kind of rotate and they don't set a starting lineup that often. In the fall, they told me I would be starting."

******

Wehrli had a stellar career at defensive back, including setting a school record by intercepting three passes in one game against Oklahoma State in 1968. But he really dazzled the crowds on special teams, where he rewrote many of the record books for kickoff and punt returns. In 1966, he ran the season-opening kickoff back 96 yards for a touchdown in a 23-7 victory over Iowa State. In 1968, he ran back six punts for 149 years against the Cyclones and set up four of the Tigers' six touchdowns.

"Certainly the interceptions and things like that are things you remember," Wehrli said. "I am proud of our strong defensive tradition throughout the '60s, and I'm proud to be part of that Devine era when Missouri football was well respected. The biggest thrill was my records returning punts and kickoffs and making big plays. I still have most of the records."

Kadlec remembers one special game against Alabama.

"We stopped them, and they had to punt," he said. "They punted to Roger, and he ran it back for a touchdown. We were offsides, so the touchdown didn't count and they got a first down. Well, we held them again, and the punter punted again to Wehrli, and he ran it back for another touchdown."

Wehrli wrapped up his All-America career with two interceptions against the Crimson Tide in the 1968 Gator Bowl.

"My senior year, Terry McMillan and Mel Gray came in, and we started to have some good, strong offensive players," he said. "We got invited to the Gator Bowl and went down there and beat Alabama 35-10. That was just a great way to end your career."

Wehrli's jersey, number 23, has been retired by the university, and he has been enshrined in the College Football Hall of Fame.

The Giant Killer

Al Onofrio led the Tigers to a record 38-41 as head coach from 1971 through 1977. Most fans, however, remember the magnitude of his victories, not the number.

Onofrio's teams were the giant killers of college football in the early and mid-1970s, knocking off such national powerhouses as Notre Dame, Alabama, Southern California and Nebraska. Before becoming head coach, Onofrio was an integral part of the success enjoyed by Dan Devine in the 1960s.

"I was with Dan Devine for three years at Arizona State," Onofrio said. "When he got the Missouri job, he asked me to go with him. Dan had a lot of success at Arizona State. When he went there, he was young, and nobody knew exactly what he would do and how he would develop. He developed very well and lost only three games in three years. When he went to Missouri in 1958 and replaced Frank Broyles, he had some experience at winning, and he was going to a good football program at an outstanding university. He did a remarkable job."

Onofrio agrees with John Kadlec that Devine's greatest strength was his organizational ability and attention to even the smallest detail.

"He knew what he wanted in a football team," Onofrio said. "He wanted to have good athletes, good discipline, good teamwork and a good attitude. He did everything he could legally to take care of the team in the best possible way. What I mean by that is that he had a dining hall for the athletes so they would get the proper food, he had the best trainers he could get, he had good orthopedic doctors and good assistant coaches.

"He was finicky about a lot of things associated with his football team. It was very important to him for the little things to be right. In that respect, he had everything planned out, and he executed it well for the years he was at Missouri. He had an uncanny ability to motivate the team at different times and in different ways. He had a way of getting a team ready to play an opponent and also to approach a season or bowl game. He was very good at that."

******

Two bowl games stand out to Onofrio from the successful decade of the 1960s. First was the 1961 Orange Bowl in which the Tigers beat Navy 21-14 while shutting down Joe Bellino, the Heisman Trophy-winning running back.

"The Navy game has to be one of our top bowl games," he said.

"In those days, Navy had outstanding football teams, and President Kennedy was in the stands. That was one of our finest games in holding Bellino to very, very few yards, although he did make a spectacular catch for a touchdown."

The second was a 35-10 victory over Alabama in the 1968 Gator Bowl.

"Bear Bryant said before the game—and he said this very seldom—that that was the best defensive team he had in a long time," Onofrio said. "They had a great passer and a good offense, and they ended up minus-67 yards for the game. Our running backs made an awful lot of yards. We completely dominated the game."

The final score was the most lopsided bowl victory in school history and Bryant's worst defeat with the Crimson Tide to that point.

******

The university promoted Onofrio to head coach for the 1971 season when Devine left for the Green Bay Packers. His first team went 1-10, but they rebounded the following season with one of the biggest upsets in school history.

Things looked bleak for the Tigers after getting beaten 62-0 by Nebraska in Lincoln.

"We really had a good team," he said, "but we ran into a buzz saw up there at Lincoln, and they scored three or four touchdowns in a span of 10 or 15 minutes. We were 35-point underdogs the next week against Notre Dame in South Bend."

No one expected what happened next.

"We went up there and played a highly ranked Notre Dame team and won 30-26," he said. "People said, 'How can you do that?' But when you look at the game itself, we played a perfect game. We didn't have a fumble, we didn't have an intercepted pass, we completed six passes and we didn't have a penalty until the last few minutes of the game when we were trying to use up time. We made four fourth-down conversions, three of them for touchdowns. We actually played a perfect game. That was a great game, and it helped our program."

Lightning struck again in 1975 in a season-opening game against No. 2 Alabama in Birmingham, Alabama.

"We were the first game of the football season, like *Monday Night Football*," Onofrio said. "It was a night football game and the only game on. We had a tremendous game and completely dominated them. That was for national exposure."

Mizzou won the game, 20-7. The next giant to fall was the University of Southern California in 1976, again in the season opener on the road.

"They lost that first game to us [46-25] and went on to be national champions," he said. "It was another complete domination, especially in the second quarter and the second half."

Onofrio also had several upsets in Big Eight Conference play.

"We beat Nebraska in 1973, the year after they beat us 62-0, and they were ranked No. 2 in the country," he said. "We beat them 13-12 in Columbia. Then we beat them in 1974 in a nationally televised game in Lincoln. After being behind 10-0 with 10 minutes left in the game, we beat them 21-10. Then the Nebraska game in 1976 was nationally televised, and they were ranked No. 2 again, but we beat them, 34-24."

******

Looking back, Onofrio believes the difficult schedules led to more injuries, which hurt the Tigers later in the season.

"In the 1975 season, we won our first three games against Alabama, Illinois and Wisconsin," he said. "Tony Galbreath hurt his heel in the win against Wisconsin, and we went up to play Michigan the next week. Keith Morrissey, our outstanding lineman, was injured and didn't play. We moved Curtis Brown, a fullback, to tailback. Michigan had a good team, and we lost that game.

"Then we lost to Colorado right at the end. We were going for a touchdown and fumbled. They had two minutes left to play and went down and scored. Some of those defeats we had were very close. Sometimes you just don't know. When it looks like you can't win, you win, and when it looks like you can't lose, you lose. That was the most disappointing thing to me when I was head coach. I wasn't disappointed in the team; I was disappointed in that we had some of those close games that we didn't win."

The University of Kansas was Onofrio's Achilles heel.

"Worst of all, we lost to Kansas six out of seven times," he said. "The last one in particular, we were only two points behind. We were on the one-yard line with about a minute left in the game and fumbled the ball, or we would have won that one."

Those losses to KU were devastating, sportswriter Bob Broeg said.

"It was a tragedy, just a sheer tragedy," he said. "If he had been 5-2 against KU rather than 1-6, which he unfortunately was, he probably could have been coaching still. That hurt him."

******

The unpredictable Tigers were fun to watch, and fans packed Faurot Field in record numbers.

"We didn't have the expanded stadium yet, so it had only 55,000 permanent seats," Onofrio said. "But during the middle 1970s, we averaged about 63,000 to 65,000 per game, and in one game, we had 69,000. We had a lot of interest in Missouri football."

******

Onofrio still keeps a close eye on Mizzou football from his Arizona home. He sees bright days ahead for the Tigers.

"I think Coach Gary Pinkel is doing an outstanding job," he said. "After a period of so many years that they were losing, they kind of lost the state of Missouri in the recruiting battles. When Pinkel came in, he and his staff hit St. Louis and the Missouri area very hard. They do a wonderful job of recruiting. They go to other

Missouri football head coach Gary Pinkel leads his team onto the field.
(AP/WWP)

states, but they make sure they know about all of the good players in the state of Missouri.

"Plus, he has a wonderful background of being under Don James as a player and a coach. He has a good system of football and knows how to coach it, and he has a staff that works hard. There is no doubt in my mind that he is going to have a winning program for many years to come."

******

Onofrio is proud to have left a good, clean program and a lot of wonderful memories.

"I consider myself lucky to have been able to coach at the University of Missouri," he said. "I was fortunate to be a member of Dan Devine's staff and very fortunate to become head football coach for those seven years. It was an extremely great 20 years for me, and I think there were many outstanding thrills, along with some disappointments. I hope the fans, when they think about me as head coach, remember that our teams always played hard and won many, many, many big games and that we brought a lot of excitement those last seven years. I enjoyed every minute of my time there."

Fifth to First in Four Weeks

Ken Downing looked at the depth chart at defensive back before his sophomore season at Mizzou, and he didn't like what he saw.

"I started out as the fifth-team Tiger [strong side] linebacker behind Ken Gregory, Steve Yount, Brad Brown and Chuck Banta," he said. "I was disenchanted and thinking about dropping out and going to Arkansas State, which had talked to me. I'm thinking, 'Man, this is not where I need to be.'"

Then, as so often happens in sports, fate took a hand.

"There were a couple of injuries, and a couple of them got into a little bit of trouble," Downing said. "The next thing I know, I'm starting the first game. I was sophomore Newcomer of the Year in the Big Eight, went on to a couple of bowl games and got to play in the Coaches' All-America game my senior year, so that was a great honor for me. I went from a fifth-team nobody to starter in about four weeks."

******

If Downing had his way, he might have been a Razorback instead of a Tiger. He played high school sports for the Hound Dogs of Aurora, Missouri, near the Arkansas border.

"I had grown up saying I was going to be a Razorback, because I was from that area," he said. "When we were sophomores, we won the state 2A championship. We had a guy from Aurora named Chuck Link who became a tailback at Mizzou and tied a record for most touchdowns in a game. They treated Chuck very well, and he showed me around when I was recruited.

"The only major college offers I had were from the University of Arkansas, Oklahoma State and Iowa State. But about three days before the signing day for letters of intent, Clay Cooper, the defensive backfield coach, shows up in Aurora unannounced and goes, 'Downing, we have one scholarship left and I have to know, do you want it or not?' I didn't even talk to my parents. I said, 'Let's sign it.' It ended up being a Cinderella story from there.

"We used to call Clay Cooper 'Daddy Coop.' He became more of a father figure in my life during those years, and I'm still very close to him."

******

Downing started for the Tigers from 1973 to 1975. He was known for stopping the run.

"The way they played me at Mizzou was more like a Tiger back than a corner, even though I played corner," he said. "I always went to the tight end side, because the Big Eight was such a running conference. I played the run better, but Coach Onofrio once said, 'You play the run well, but you never got beaten on a pass for a touchdown, either.'"

******

Downing will never forget the season opener his junior season.

"The biggest game I can remember is opening the 1975 season against Alabama on Monday night TV," he said. "We won, 20 to seven, and I was named Chevrolet Player of the Game and got the scholarship award. That was quite an honor.

"That was the year we were called the giant killers. We beat everybody who was ranked, but Kansas, Iowa State and some of those people sneaked by us."

Downing played in two bowls, the 1972 Fiesta Bowl against Arizona State and the 1973 Sun Bowl against Auburn. Mizzou won both games.

"I remember that in the Fiesta Bowl they wanted to make me a punt and kickoff returner for the last game of the year," he said. "That was the only time I came close to thinking I was breaking one. On a kickoff return, I ran it out about 60 yards but got tackled at the end."

******

Downing played briefly for the New Orleans Saints and Chicago Bears, then five years with the Ottawa Roughriders of the Canadian Football League. After retiring from football, he became a chiropractor and runs a successful practice in Kansas City with a number of professional athletes as patients.

"What stands out to me is being a three-year starter, getting a degree from the university and preparing for what I am doing now," he said. "I didn't make Kodak All-America, but I made Coaches' All-America. I hope I am remembered as a well-disciplined, hard-hitting, smart player. I was proud to be a Tiger."

******

Members of Coach Onofrio's team held a reunion during the 2002 football season, and Downing attended with his wife.

"My wife asked, 'How long has it been since you've seen these guys?' I said, 'Since 1976 for some of them. And she said, 'I can't believe the camaraderie. It's like you guys were together yesterday.'

"Through blood, sweat and tears for four years, you get to know people inside and out. You're in it as group, so you build a camaraderie I have never achieved any other place, even in the professional ranks."

Hometown Hero

Growing up in Columbia in the 1960s, John Moseley hung out with kids named Kadlec, Devine and Onofrio—as in John Kadlec, Dan Devine and Al Onofrio.

"I played football at Hickman High School with two of Coach Onofrio's sons," he said. "I think he's a good man and a real gentleman."

It was a time when Tiger football was king in mid-Missouri. "In Columbia back then, there were more people at the football games than the population of the town," Moseley said.

Moseley, a defensive back and running back in high school, wanted to be part of the tradition. Several small state schools made scholarship offers, but not the Tigers.

"I decided I wanted to play at Missouri," he said. "Actually, I think my mother went over and spoke to [defensive backfield coach] Clay Cooper, unbeknownst to me. I didn't get a scholarship offer, so I walked on."

It didn't take Moseley long to learn that the numbers were stacked against him.

"We had like 119 people who tried out in the fall of 1970," he said. "At that time, they also gave something like 44 scholarships. I broke my ankle in practice, so there was a lot of apprehension."

However, Moseley made the freshman squad, playing at both receiver and defensive back. He got to know Devine before he left to coach the Green Bay Packers.

"He didn't leave until February or so," Devine said. "We had a couple of meetings with him. Coach Devine was very charming when dealing with someone one on one. He saw me a couple of times on crutches and took the time to visit with me. He did all the right things to fire you up.

"Now in a meeting, he was a different guy. Basically, everyone was afraid of Coach Devine. "

******

Al Onofrio took over as head coach and offered Moseley a scholarship after spring practice.

"We had great senior defensive backs in Lorenzo Brinkley and Henry Stuckey," he said. "Mel Gray had graduated, and they were short on receivers. Before the game against Army, the coaches called me in on Tuesday morning and said, 'We're moving you to receiver. You're going to dress and probably play.' I worked at receiver for the rest of that week. We went to West Point, and I played at wide receiver. It was pretty wild. I then went back to defensive back and started at cornerback my junior and senior years."

Moseley was regarded as a hard hitter despite his size.

"I'm five foot eight and 160 pounds or so, but I took a lot of pride in my tackling," he said. "I was strong on the pass, and Kenny Downing was our guy on the run. I talk to guys now that I played against, and they say, 'Man, we hated to play you guys.'

"We had kind of a reading defense where our front eight's first assignment was to smack the guy across from you, try to determine which way he's going to take you and go the other way. We were a tough team. That was the era of the wishbone, and I would be on the receiver. Clay put me on Johnny Rodgers when we played Nebraska, and I usually went with the best receiver. I was not as good of a cover guy as Deion Sanders, but I was a better tackler."

******

As with many of his former teammates, the 30-26 victory at Notre Dame in 1972 seems just like yesterday.

"Notre Dame was every bit as big then as it is now, if not bigger," he said.

"On Sunday afternoons, Lindsey Nelson and Paul Hornung always did snippets of the Notre Dame game on television."

Things looked bleak for the Tigers before their trip to South Bend.

"We had gotten beat 62-0 the week before by Nebraska," he said. "We thought we were good football players and everything, but when you get beat 62-0 and then beat Notre Dame, all of a sudden you start thinking you are a good team. And then we were a good team and went to a bowl game."

Moseley recalls playing well against the Fighting Irish.

"You do your own job when you are in a team atmosphere like that and depend on the other guy to do his job," he said. "I thought I played very well. We played man to man and a little zone, and because we did that, teams often would put their biggest receiver on me. I covered their big tight end that they would split out, and I don't remember anyone catching a pass on me.

"That Notre Dame game was a big deal, because we had been 1-10 the previous season, and that really turned things around."

The Tigers earned bids to the Fiesta Bowl after his junior season and the Sun Bowl following his senior year. "I actually had good games in both bowls," Moseley said. "It's funny how the game you have taints your memories, but it's fun when you do well."

******

Moseley will long be remembered as the only Missouri Tiger to go from walk-on to All-America. The honor becomes more significant as the years go by, he said.

"We were going into a team meeting, and Bill Callahan, the sports information director, called to me and said, 'Hey, come over here.' I thought, 'What have I done now?' He said, 'I wanted to let you know you've been named All-America by the football writers.' When you are living it, everything happens so fast. But I'm very proud of that. I also was co-captain in my senior year, and that was enough for me. I started spring ball in my freshman year as the No. 8 wide receiver, and there was no way I could have accomplished what I did without Coach Cooper taking an interest in me."

******

Moseley, who played two years for Honolulu in the World Football League, continues to call Columbia home. Former teammates frequently give him a call when passing through town.

"It's funny," he said, "but in the biggest game of my college career, I don't remember who the Notre Dame quarterback was. But the important thing is the people I interacted with on my own team over years. Missouri was a different place in the 1970s. We didn't have weightlifting, we didn't have the great facilities like a lot of places have, but we had some tough guys who played tough defense. I hope I am remembered as a team player who was all about trying to win games."

Doubling Up in Football and Baseball

Many players have played more than one sport at Missouri, but few have had more success than Phil Bradley.

Bradley quarterbacked the exciting football teams of the late 1970s and finished his career with a conference-record 6,459 yards of total offense. If anything, he was even better in baseball. He went on to a successful career as a major-league outfielder, and Mizzou retired his uniform number during the 2003 season. Coming out of high school in Illinois, he wanted to pursue both sports.

"I was looking to go play two sports somewhere," he said. "I knew they were interested in me, and I knew the history of Missouri, that they played competitive schedules and were a successful program. I think I was recruited as a football player who had intentions of playing baseball.

"It's a big challenge; you can't kid yourself. But when you play three sports in high school, it's kind of what you know. The time management and commitment aspects were normal to me."

******

Bradley was a key player in one of the most talented groups of athletes in school history.

"The class of 1977 was me, Johnnie Poe, Eric

Wright, Wendell Ray, Bill Whittaker, James Wilder and Jerome Sally," he said. "I would say that close to 90 percent of those guys had NFL careers—not just an appearance in the NFL. I don't know what history would show, but I would be very surprised if one class did any more in the NFL than our class did."

******

Bradley believed in setting his sights high.

"For me, the two biggest games were Oklahoma and Nebraska," he said. "They were the two best teams in the conference. I'm not from Missouri, and not to insult the people from Kansas, but in my opinion, the rivals were the two biggest teams in the conference. We beat Nebraska one time and never beat Oklahoma. In three of my four years, we gave Oklahoma a competitive game. All four years, the games against Nebraska were competitive. The game in 1980 was a pretty close game also for a while.

"We played in two Liberty Bowls and a Hall of Fame Bowl and won two out of three. We got an opportunity to play George Rogers, the Heisman Trophy winner from South Carolina. 1978 was the biggest accomplishment bowl-wise, because we were kind of down and out. In weeks seven and eight, we had bad losses, and it looked like were down and out, then beat Kansas. We came back and beat Nebraska the last week of the season to give us a record of 7-4."

******

Bradley played for both Al Onofrio and Warren Powers. All in all, he is proud of what his teams accomplished.

"We had three winning seasons out of four and played in three bowl games," he said. "I had the opportunity to play with a lot of good football players. When I left in 1980, I was the all-time total offense leader in the Big Eight Conference.

"I think I am remembered as the quarterback of the last good era of Missouri football. I played on three teams that had winning records, and it has taken Missouri 20 years to get two winning seasons. When you are in the midst of it, you don't think about how you will be looked upon by history. Things run in cycles."

******

Helping revive the Tiger baseball team may have been an even more impressive feat.

"We won the Big Eight tournament in 1980, and that was the last time they won a conference tournament," Bradley said. "We didn't have big-name players. In the three years I was there, I was the only guy who got drafted. The program was about being competitive. In the three years I played there, the team averaged 45 wins a season. That speaks for itself."

******

Bradley has played baseball in cities from Baltimore to Chicago to Seattle, but he still calls Columbia home.

"The choice I made was the right choice 26 years ago, and it's the right choice today," he said. "I took advantage of the opportunities I had. I was fortunate to play with for good people, with good people and against good people. Those were the three things I wanted to do when I came here."

Right Place at the Right Time

Michael Jones may not be the most famous football player from Mizzou, but he undoubtedly was involved in one of the most unforgettable plays.

Jones, as a linebacker for the St. Louis Rams in Super Bowl XXXIV, tackled Tennessee receiver Kevin Dyson on the one-yard line, preserving a 23-16 victory by the Rams. Ironically, Jones never played a single down of defense for the Tigers.

"I played both ways in high school," Jones said. "Of course, I wanted to be a running back at Mizzou, but when they recruited me, they never really said what position I would play. What happened was we ran the wishbone offense, and one of the players got hurt. They moved me from fullback to a running back, and I was a running back the rest of the time.

"Each year, there was talk about moving me over to defense, but it never happened."

******

Jones followed the great Missouri teams of the late 1970s while growing up in Kansas City.

"Phil Bradley, James Wilder, Eric Wright and all of those guys were there," he said. "As a Kansas City kid, we also were close to Kansas, but there were good teams at Missouri when I was a youngster. They went on a little downslide when I was in high school, but they still came to recruit me."

Building a Family

Relationships have always been important to Elijah Blackwell. One of the reasons he chose to play at Mizzou was to be near his family in St. Louis.

"I played tight end and linebacker at St. Louis Central High School," he said, "but when I got to Mizzou, I played linebacker and a little defensive end. I was being recruited by all of the Big Eight schools, but the reason I picked Mizzou was that it was really close to home and my parents could come to my games."

He also considers his teammates part of that extended family.

"A lot of the guys, like Demetrious Johnson, Kevin Potter and Curt Thomas, played against each other in high school," he said. "Once we got up there to Mizzou, we became just like a family."

******

Blackwell graduated from high school early and arrived on campus in January 1979. He was in awe of the talent in the football program.

"Guys like Wendell Ray, Eric Wright and Lester Dickey were two years ahead of me," he said. "There were probably 10 guys from those teams who were drafted by the NFL."

Blackwell believes the friendships off the field contributed to the success on the field.

"All of us were close," he said. "The whole team as a unit worked together and played hard, but we also went out and had a good time together. The whole team stuck together. That's why we had so many bowl games, because of that camaraderie."

The Tigers enjoyed so much postseason success that fans began to take it for granted, he said.

"We went to the Liberty Bowl, Hall of Fame Bowl and Tangerine Bowl, so the majority of the years I was there, we did go to some type of bowl game," he said. "We definitely did take it for granted. Now you see it's really not like that at the time."

******

More than two decades later, Blackwell still is reaping the benefits of playing for coach Warren Powers and the University of Missouri.

"The biggest thing was that I had the chance to advance to the next level and play for the Minnesota Vikings," he said. "Mizzou taught me a good work ethic, and it was a great school. I definitely made the right choice.

"Football definitely has helped me in life. Period. Mizzou has blessed my life, and it has blessed me with lifelong friends who have been watching my back."

******

Like many former players, the long struggle to rebuild the football program has been painful for Blackwell to watch. He sees better days ahead and believes players such as him can be part of the success.

"I'm excited," he said. "Coach Gary Pinkel is bringing all of the former players on the sidelines. If you are just driving through Columbia and call the athletics department, Coach Pinkel is going to treat you as if you are still going to school there. The way he treats the former players is unheard of and something that Mizzou never did. That is going to turn into victories."

Success On and Off the Field

Demetrious Johnson has enough accolades to fill several scrapbooks. He was an All-Conference defensive back at Mizzou and enjoyed a long professional career with the Detroit Lions, Miami Dolphins and San Diego Chargers. His proudest possession, however, is his diploma from the University of Missouri.

"My biggest accomplishment at the University of Missouri was graduating in four years," he said. "It was a huge deal, because I promised my mother and family I was going to get a degree. When I look at the other big accomplishment, it was becoming an All-Conference player in a very difficult conference. Coming out of obscurity, where nobody really gave me an opportunity to be there and do well, I ended up starting, becoming an All-Big Eight player and drafted in the NFL draft."

Johnson, who is from St. Louis, chose Missouri over the University of Nebraska.

"I was recruited by Bill 'Thunder' Thornton, the running backs coach," he said. "I wanted to stay close to home so my family could come up and support me and be part of my growing experience at college."

Johnson joined the football program in 1979, when it was enjoying a great deal of success under coach Warren Powers. Cracking the starting lineup was a major challenge.

"I think the thing I'm most proud of as an athlete at the University of Missouri is becoming a starter and being able to play when the competition was so great," he said. "It was hard. If you weren't performing, you weren't playing. Man, just to be able to start at the University of Missouri with its great tradition was very exciting to me.'"

******

Johnson, like many of his teammates, believes Powers was underappreciated by Mizzou fans. All he did was compile a record of 46-33-3. "What Warren Powers did for the university during his time there was unbelievable," he said. "It has not been duplicated yet."

Powers also built a deep and talented coaching staff that helped Johnson hone his skills.

"I had one of the best defensive back coaches I've ever seen, Zavan Yaralian," he said. "When you look at when he was coaching, there were a number of defensive backs going to the NFL. This guy was hard, he was disciplined, he made you become committed, he was one of the best coaches I ever had—and I'm talking about high school, college and the pros. He became defensive coordinator for the New Orleans Saints and also was secondary coach for the New York Giants and Chicago Bears. He really did well."

******

Victories against Oklahoma have been few and far between for the Tigers, but Johnson participated in a 19-14 upset of the No. 15 Sooners in 1981.

"My biggest win was beating Oklahoma," he said. "I caught the quarterback from behind without letting him score a touchdown. They were ranked, and we beat them. Faurot Field was packed—you couldn't even see the M on the hill. Just the excitement and pageantry... it was the most exciting thing that ever happened to me."

******

Johnson also is proud of his individual accomplishments, which don't always show up on the stat sheets.

"When Mizzou fans mention my name, one thing I want them to understand was that I was a very intense, committed player," he said. "I was a very good hitter and tackler who was determined to work hard and win at the University of Missouri. I left it all on the field and worked hard every game. I wasn't afraid of competition, and I looked forward to the big games.

"When they look back in my career, I want fans to say, 'You know what? He was one of the better defensive backs to come out of here because of his ability to play hard at all times.'"

******

Johnson has led a successful life, both on and off the field. But he has yet to find anything to replace the satisfaction of being part of a team.

"When I played in the NFL, the money was good, and in college, the games were good," he said. "But the thing you miss sorely in the business world is that no other entity in this world develops great friendships like sports. That's what I miss the most—the locker room talks, the jokes, the things we said about one another, getting up and going to bed together, eating together and going on the road together.

"When you crossed that line, you became a family. You strapped it up together, you looked at one another and said, 'You know what? This is what it's all about.' It superseded race, it superseded economic status, it superseded religious beliefs. It made you appreciate one another, and it made you accept one another.

"That's what I miss most, that camaraderie, that appreciation, when I can look at a guy across the line and he's sweating, tears coming out of his eyes like mine, you're mirroring yourself and you're mirroring that person. That's what you miss, because the world doesn't give that one-for-all, all-for-one attitude."

A Starring Role

Conrad Goode must have been destined to be an All-America offensive tackle at Missouri. His father, Conrad Hitchler, was an All-American at the same position in 1962, and his stepfather was an All-American at the University of Kentucky. However, Goode almost wound up playing in the Big Ten, not the Big Eight.

"I played high school football at Parkway Central in St. Louis," he said. "I could have pretty much gone anywhere in the Midwest. I took my recruiting trips to Michigan, Ohio State, Notre Dame, Wisconsin, Missouri and Georgia Tech. When Missouri first came in the picture, I was leaning toward Ohio State or Michigan. I was pretty close to going one of those two places, but my last recruiting trip was Missouri. I got to know Mike Price and Warren Powers, and they changed my mind. My stepfather was an All-American in Kentucky and grew up there, and he said there is something about going to the state school, a loyalty that will mean a lot more to you down the line."

Goode knew exactly what he wanted to accomplish in his four years.

"I was the type of guy who set a goal each year," he said. "My freshman year, it was to make the traveling squad. My sophomore year, it was to start. And then it was to become All-Big Eight, All-America and turn pro. I kind of took it one step at a time."

******

Goode played in one of the last successful eras of Missouri football before a long dry spell. His teams played Purdue in the 1980 Liberty Bowl, Southern Mississippi in the 1981 Tangerine Bowl and BYU in the 1983 Holiday Bowl. There also were some memorable regular-season games in those years.

"Four games really stick out in my mind," he said. "First would have to be my sophomore year. We started the season 3-0 and went down and played Mississippi State. They were ranked about No. 5 in the nation at the time. We went down to Jackson and beat them. The same year, we beat Oklahoma in Columbia for the first time in a long time. The fans tore down the goalposts and carried them back to the bars. That was pretty exciting.

"Then my senior year I was fortunate enough to be voted co-captain with Jay Wilson. We opened in Columbia against the University of Illinois, and the excitement was in the air, all the pomp and circumstance of college football. We came out for warmups in our old uniforms that we had worn the previous three years. In the locker room, they had these new uniforms waiting for us. So between warmups and kickoff, we went into the locker room and changed into these new uniforms. They were bright new colors, at a time when everyone was going to neon bright colors.

"So Jay and I walked out of the locker room for the coin flip before the rest of the team, and we're walking through the tunnel, and the fans see the new uniforms, and the whole place just goes crazy. They are screaming and going nuts and everything. I think it's probably the closest feeling I've ever had to being a rock star. The whole stadium erupted, and Jay and I are pumping our fists. We won the coin flip and went out and beat Illinois. It kind of set the tone for our senior year.

"Fourth, later that season, we beat Oklahoma again in Columbia. Those four games really stick out in my mind."

******

Conrad Hitchler found out from the sports information director that he had been named All-America. Conrad Goode learned it from a Columbia radio station.

"I was hoping and praying I was named," he said. "I was driving back from practice for the Holiday Bowl and heard it on the radio. By the time I got to my apartment, there were three or four messages on my machine. That's how I heard about it. I couldn't believe it."

*****

The New York Giants drafted Goode after his senior season. That led to finding an undiscovered talent and a second career after football.

"When I was playing ball for the Giants, one off season a theatrical agent who was a football fan was flipping through the program and saw my picture in it," he said. "He thought I had an interesting look and called me up and wanted to know if I was interested in auditioning for a commercial. I didn't know anything about acting at the time. I told him that, and he goes, 'Just go over and be yourself.'

"I get to this massive cattle call in New York City, and I'm going, 'What am I doing here? There are 350 people, and I have to wait an hour.' But I get in there and yuk it up a little bit, and I got the job. I thought, 'Wow, this is a lot of fun.' So the agent called me and booked a couple more commercials and a couple of music videos. I did a TV special. I just kind of fell in love with the craft and the process of filmmaking. It kind of took over.

"I was an art major at Missouri and have always been kind of an artistic person. I just started studying acting and writing, and it felt like a natural segue. Now I think I was more of an actor playing football than a football player turned actor."

Goode has acted in 18 feature films, including *Anger Management, Don't Say a Word, Me, Myself & Irene,* and *ConAir.*

"In the beginning, I was always playing the heavy," he said. "Now I'm getting the opportunity to play a nicer type of person."

******

Goode has led an exciting life, playing professional football in New York and Tampa Bay and now acting in Los Angeles. But few experiences rival his days as a Tiger.

"I look back on my four years at Missouri as four of the best years of my life," he said. "I have nothing but fond memories of great friendships and good times. I went out there and enjoyed the game, I enjoyed wearing the black and gold and I had a good time doing it. I'm thankful for the opportunity to go to the University of Missouri."

Born to Be a Tiger

Not a lot of Division I coaches came around Washington, Missouri, to recruit running back Brock Olivo. That's good, because they would have been wasting their time.

"I did not even consider other schools," he said. "It was only a matter of whether Mizzou would offer me a scholarship or not. If not, I would have joined the team as a walk-on. I was supposed to be a Tiger. The only selling point for Mizzou was the fact that it was my home state university. If I had grown up in Montana, I'd have gone to Montana State. There was nothing more rewarding than sliding that helmet on and running through the visitors' tunnel knowing we represented the state of Missouri—that was pride as I know it."

Olivo started the trend of top-notch Missouri players such as Devin West, Corby Jones and Justin Smith staying in-state, which led to a resurgence of the program in the mid- to late 1990s.

"I remember growing up always hearing about Nebraska and Illinois and seeing Notre Dame on TV and waiting for the day when I would see Ol' Mizzou on that same level," he said. "Then I would see the rosters from the neighboring state universities, and there would be six or eight Missouri kids. This was the knife in my heart. I always wonder how they could abandon their home state to wear someone else's colors."

Devin West
(AP/WWP)

Olivo is proud to have played a part in convincing Jones to become a Tiger.

"Two weeks before Corby's visit to the campus, I was called into my running back coach's office," he said. "My coach at the time was the late Curtis Jones, Corby's father. He said, 'Brocko, you will host Corby on his visit, and nothing would make me happier than to see him the in black and gold.' No pressure.

"So I remember sitting next to Corby in the wee hours of that Sunday morning and him turning to me and saying, 'You know, Brock, Nebraska wants me to play quarterback and they are bringing me in next week—I don't know what to do.'

"Here I was with one of the most highly touted recruits in the last 20 years in the state of Missouri, he obviously is torn between staying home or going for the big show, and all I can come up with is 'Well, Corb, you don't look good in red.' That conversation took place at the Broadway Diner, and about 10 hours later, Corby Jones was a Missouri Tiger."

******

Olivo was legendary for a self-imposed workout regimen that would have put Rocky Balboa to shame. But no one would have imagined that he would finish his career as the school's all-time leading rusher, with 3,026 career yards. He also was honored as national special teams Player of the Year after his senior season. But what he remembers best are the big victories and heart-breaking losses.

"The biggest victory of my career was the 1997 win over the then-No. 12 Oklahoma State Cowboys," he said. The Tigers won that shootout in Stillwater, Oklahoma, 51-50 in two overtimes.

"Two words enter my mind when I think of that game—Ricky Ross," he said. "If ever a single play defined a career, it was Ricky's touchdown catch in the corner of the end zone with less than a minute left. The game went into overtime, and we came out on top. I get chills, because I cannot recall a time when I felt so rewarded, so relieved and so proud to be a part of something. It was from that moment on that we felt like contenders. There was an incredible feeling in the air. We had arrived, and the Missouri Tigers were back on the map."

Two games later, Olivo was part of one of the most bizarre losses in school history. Top-ranked Nebraska came to Columbia and won in overtime after a controversial play at the end of regulation, when one player kicked the ball to another for a game-tying touchdown.

"Thanks to ESPN Classic, that game will never be forgotten," he said. "Although it was a loss in the books, it gave us even more of a boost of confidence. In a weird and twisted way, I am almost glad now that it fell the way it did. I fear we would have been labeled lucky, when instead that title now rests on Nebraska's conscience.

"I can still hear the MIZ-ZOU chant from that game. I have never seen Faurot Field so electrified and yet so calming. At this point, we had the nation's attention. Our ultimate goal that year was to go to a bowl game, and we made it happen."

******

The 1997 Plymouth Holiday Bowl was the Tigers' first bowl appearance in 14 seasons. Olivo carried the ball seven times for 37 yards in the 35-24 loss to Colorado State.

"I remember being at the 1997 Holiday Bowl press conference and listening to [Coach] Larry Smith and [athletics director] Joe Castiglione and thinking, 'Is this really happening? Ol' Mizzou in a bowl game?'" he said.

"The period between the regular season and the bowl game was, in a word, surreal. Press conferences, award ceremonies and instant celebrity status for the entire team made for a roller coaster of emotions.

"It would not hit me that we did it until the plane touched down in sunny San Diego and it was almost 100 degrees. That was my proudest moment as a Tiger, to step off that plane as a representative of the state of Missouri in a moment of glory. We just overcame 15 years of adversity. We were all smiles. I don't have a favorite moment, because I remember every single minute of that trip. Just being there and being recognized as one of college football's elite teams was enough.

"The game was an incredible production, our fans were absolutely brilliant, we lost the game and it did not matter. I love our fans, and that did it for me, to see them by the thousands supporting us far from home and welcoming us back at the airport on our arrival. I will never forget that moment. I love our fans."

******

Olivo is excited that his jersey number soon will be only the seventh to be retired in school history.

"There is no doubt that the jersey retirement will be the greatest reward ever bestowed upon me," he said. "In one way, I am so proud of what took place at Mizzou and the things we were able to accomplish. But in another weird sense, I wish I were just another one of many incredibly hard workers and national award winners, because that is what makes a program. The awards are simply the proof or the aftermath of what took place on the playing field.

"Any award I ever won is a reflection of each and every Tiger I shared the field with, from the walk-ons who would run hills with me at five o'clock in the morning to All-Americans in the trenches up front. It is better this way, because not everyone gets noticed. Some players slip though the cracks, and it is up to the fortunate players like myself who fall in the limelight to make sure they are noticed.

"I was simply a good football player on a good football team."

******

Olivo has a strong appreciation of the history of Missouri football and is proud to be part of the long tradition.

"Being mentioned among the likes of Johnny Roland and James Wilder is just as good as any award one could receive," he said.

"Nowadays, with college football's rich history, it is interesting to take today's players and compare them with yesteryear's, because there have been so many advances in the game, on and off the field.

"Did Johnny Roland's fullback weigh 280 pounds and bench-press 500 pounds? Did James Wilder play behind three All-Americans? Did the running backs from the '30s and '40s have the facilities to really improve themselves physically, and did they even have the opportunity to scout other teams and learn in the football 'classroom?'

"However, with a name such as Harry Ice, one wouldn't have to do much more than sign his name to be golden. As long as college football is alive and evolving, there will be this incredible story line made up of individual players, some on peaks and some in the valleys, but all having contributed to the story.

"My part was small, but we peaked as a team at the right moment, and I was recognized as a leader of that moment, just like Johnny Roland of his time and James Wilder of his. And as for Harry Ice, I got to shake his hand, and I'll accept that as my reward for doing my part."

A Nose for the Quarterback

The Tigers have had their share of big players, and they have had speedy ones. But none combined size and quickness like Justin Smith.

Smith set school records for most sacks in a season (11) and in a career (22.5). He accomplished those feats in just three seasons before joining the Cincinnati Bengals as the fourth overall pick in the 2001 NFL draft.

Just as Brock Olivo before him, the Jefferson City High School product never considered going elsewhere.

"I always liked Mizzou and always thought it would be awesome to play there," he said. "I went to a few football games when I was a kid, and I never really strayed off that path.

"My big deal was, if you're good enough to play Division I football, you'd might as well stay in your home state and play. I always tried to tell guys that in recruiting visits, but unfortunately it doesn't always happen. You look at all the talent that came out of Missouri, and you definitely could have been a powerhouse."

******

Like many great players, Smith played his best in the biggest games.

"The game I got most fired up for was Nebraska," he said. "There was something about those guys, man. I just wanted to beat them so bad. Mizzou hadn't beaten them in 20-some years, and those were the guys I wanted to beat. We had a super team that year but ended up losing. We were able to get down there with two opportunities to score on the last drive and had passes dropped in the end zone. Man, that summed up our whole career with Nebraska."

The Tigers lost that game in Lincoln, 45-38 in overtime. There would be other tough losses.

"My freshman year, we lost some games that stand out more than the ones we won," he said. "When K-State was there with Maurice Bishop, we lost to them in overtime. We beat Oklahoma that year, and we should have beaten Nebraska at Nebraska. It's more the losses you remember."

******

When Missouri beat West Virginia 34-31 in the 1998 Insight.com Bowl, it was the Tigers' first bowl victory since the 1981 Tangerine Bowl.

"It was really special for the seniors," Smith said. "That was the year Corby's dad died, and we were playing for Curtis Jones. It just really came together for everybody, a special year and a special game. We were able to beat a good team. Unfortunately, we were not able to carry that momentum on further. But that was definitely fun that whole year and that experience."

******

There are legends about the Missouri coaching staff having to kick Smith out of the weight room.

"Everybody worked hard," Smith said. "Brock kind of laid the foundation for that, and everybody followed. It was a heart-and-soul deal. We were able to make something out of not a whole lot of talent there. What I remember from my career is just playing with the guys, sweating with them all year, working out and then being on the field playing with them."

******

By his junior season, Smith had the attention of every offensive coordinator in the nation and frequently was double-teamed. Even so, he managed to fight his way through to the quarterback.

"You take it as a challenge and see it as a sign of respect," he said. "But at the same time, you're upset that they won't just play you regularly. That's the way it goes, but I have no regrets about Mizzou. I learned more from the losses than from the wins, anyway.

"My whole deal the whole time I was there was to outwork everybody and be better. I think that first group of guys Larry Smith brought in, like Brock and Ron Janes, all those guys really worked hard, and you saw that as a freshman. I took that and ran with it. I went off their example, and I still live and die by it."

12 *Gage*

Justin Gage crammed about as much into a four-year career at Mizzou as it is possible to do.

In football, he played quarterback for Larry Smith and blossomed as an All-Conference wide receiver under Gary Pinkel. He gave Norm Stewart valuable minutes on the basketball floor and went to an Elite Eight with Quin Snyder.

Justin Gage (12) rallies the troops.
(Getty Images)

"I enjoyed competing every chance I got and being around a lot of great friends," he said.

Gage is especially thankful for the people who have contributed to his success, beginning with his parents, Al and Ernestine Gage of Jefferson City.

"My parents led me in the right direction, taught me right from wrong and helped me stay out of trouble," he said. "Coach Ron Cole [of Jefferson City High School] helped keep me stay active in sports and in the weight room instead of hanging out with the wrong crowd. In college, Coach Pinkel and Coach Snyder taught me different concepts of the game and what it takes to be on your own and become successful in life."

Although Gage enjoyed playing for Smith's staff, he would have loved to have been able to play for Pinkel all four years.

"Coach Pinkel knows a lot about the game of football, and he pushed me to be my best," he said. "He taught me not only about football and preparation but what it takes to be a winner. The Mizzou staff absolutely prepared me to take my game to the next level."

Gage ended his football career with 200 receptions for 2,704 yards and 18 touchdowns.

******

Gage gave up his hoop dreams after his junior year to concentrate on football and preparing for the NFL draft. However, he believes basketball contributed to his football success.

Justin Gage
(AP/WWP)

"I'm really happy I played basketball," he said. "It was a good opportunity to make it to the Elite Eight, travel and do all the things we did. It just gave me that winning edge that I bring over to the football field.

"I really appreciated the opportunity just to go to college, get an education and play basketball and football free of charge. Plus, it took a lot of stress off my family to find a way for me to get through school and do something I love."

******

Gage's Sundays now are committed to the Chicago Bears. But on Saturday afternoons, his thoughts turn to Faurot Field.

"I would like to be remembered for my hard work and my competitive nature," he said. "Every time I played, I gave it my all.

"Missouri is home. Regardless of where I am and what I am doing, I'll always be a Tiger."

No Limits

Players such as Johnny Roland, Phil Bradley and Brock Olivo represent the proud past of Missouri football. Quarterback Brad Smith represents its exciting future.

Not only has no freshman at Mizzou ever had such a successful rookie season, few freshmen in NCAA history can approach what he accomplished in 2002. After beating out senior Kirk Farmer, Smith became the first freshman in school history to open the season at quarterback.

Smith was under center when the Tigers began the 2002 season with a convincing 33-20 victory over the University of Illinois in the Edward Jones Dome in St. Louis. He passed for 152 yards and ran for 138.

"I told many people behind the scenes in our program that this guy is a remarkably talented athlete with remarkable poise," Coach Gary Pinkel said after the game.

Smith went on to log season numbers that would be a decent career for some players. He passed for 2,333 yards while rushing for 1,029. That made him only the second player in NCAA Division I history to pass for 2,000 yards and rush for 1,000 in the same season.

He earned numerous postseason accolades:

•Honorable mention All-America by CNNSI.com and *College Football News*.

•First team freshman All-America by the Football

Brad Smith
(AP/WWP)

Writers Association of America, *The Sporting News*, *College Football News*, and Rivals.com.

•Big 12 Conference offensive freshman of the year and honorable mention All-Conference by the Big 12 coaches.

Nearly as impressive as the statistics is the way Smith led the team with poise, confidence and humility. He made a good impression on Michael Jones, a former Tiger and Super Bowl hero.

"He's a great talent, but even better than that, he's very humble," Jones said. "Sometimes you think a guy with that type of talent would be a little arrogant, but he's very down to earth. You wouldn't even know he's Brad Smith when you walked by him. He's not a guy who stands out, but when you watch him on the field, he's a heck of a football player."

******

Smith comes from a close-knit family—both biological and extended—in Youngstown, Ohio. He talks daily with his mother, Sherri, and she attends most of his games.

"What she impressed on me most is to have integrity in everything you do," he said. "A lot of people today are cutting corners, not doing things right and making excuses for things they know aren't right. But if you always strive to do the right thing and stay on the straight path, it's going to work out."

Sherri Smith is an administrative assistant at Mount Calvary Pentecostal Church in Youngstown. Faith plays an important role in Brad Smith's life.

"One of the most important things when I made my decision about college was to have a Christian coach and atmosphere," he said. "Without that atmosphere, it could mess everything up. Leading up to the season, with the hard work we put in, it was good to know God has been helping me. He helps us stay focused and keep our heads on straight. God has definitely helped us."

******

The leaders at Mount Calvary played a role in steering Smith to Mizzou. Pinkel and his staff zeroed in on Smith early when they were at the University of Toledo. They kept after him when Pinkel accepted the Missouri job.

"Coach Pinkel going to Missouri was a plus for me," Smith said. "Missouri is in the Big 12, and Toledo is in the Mid-American Conference. I wanted to go to as big of a school as I could. I liked the tradition and the size of Missouri compared to other schools that recruited me. Academics also was very important to me, along with football and my teammates. I want to do equally well in my academics and have a good support system."

While Smith was starring at Chaney High School in Youngstown, Jim Tressel was winning national championships across town at Youngstown State. He also had his eye on Smith.

"Jim Tressel came to my house and recruited me two weeks before he went to Ohio State," Smith said.

Brad Smith celebrates a touchdown during Missouri's
season-opening victory over Illinois in 2002.
(AP/WWP)

"My mom had asked him if he would be leaving, and he didn't think so at the time. I didn't commit and came to Missouri."

Pinkel's last hurdle was a meeting with church leadership.

"Coach Matt Eberflus and Coach Pinkel came to visit, and we gave them a tour of the church," Smtih said. "My pastor called us into the office, and Coach Pinkel talked about the team and what his vision was. Then I went out and my mom and some elders of the church went in and asked him about what was going on.

"When I went back in, my pastor said it would be OK for me to go to Missouri. I was interested in coming here, and I knew it was the right decision."

******

Smith was eager to play right away but now is thankful that he was redshirted as a freshman

"I just went to practice and tried to get better every day," he said. "It helped me get bigger, faster, stronger and smarter and learn the offense better. I think it's a plus for any player to redshirt to get the feel for the game and be out there on the field and just observe everything before you actually go out there."

Smith soon became a workout room legend who drew comparisons to Olivo and Justin Smith. He spent long winter nights tossing footballs into trash cans in the training facility.

"It's just something I do," he said. "The more I work on things, the better things work out. I hope to put an example out there for guys who may be on the borderline to work harder."

******

That hard work paid off when Pinkel selected Smith to start the season. Smith appreciates the way Farmer handled the demotion.

"Kirk was as great as he could be when he was put in that situation," he said. "He was always respectful and never tried to put me down. He was always there to support and help us. He helped me in the meetings and was always prepared to play. That speaks a lot about him. I'm sure he'll do well in anything he does."

******

Veteran Tiger fans were amazed at Smith's composure, but it was no big deal to him.

"It's just a game, and I've played it since I was young," he said. "Every time I go out there, it's relaxing for me. It's therapy for me to out there and try to make plays and be there with my teammates. I give it everything I have to win the game. I let everything go and have fun."

Smith is quiet by nature, but he is not afraid to light a fire under his teammates.

"When I'm on the field, I focus and try to do whatever it takes, whether it's raising my voice or just going out there and making a play," he said.

"It was really easy for me. The guys on the team really were helping me with their words and had confidence in me. That's the most important thing, when they can trust you to go out there and do the right thing and lead the team."

Perhaps the only person not surprised by Smith's freshman season was Smith himself. "I expect to play well, to do well and make big plays," he said. "That's just what I expect to do."

******

A portrait of Frank Sinkwich, winner of the 1942 Heisman Trophy, hangs proudly at his alma mater, Chaney High School. The school would like nothing better than to hang a portrait of a second famous graduate. Smith, however, is taking the hype in stride.

"I'm excited about it," he said. "It pushes me that much more to step in there and fill that role of what people expect. I love expectations. The higher you set them, the harder I try to reach them."

Smith certainly has set high expectations for the rest of his career at Mizzou.

"I just want to win," he said. "I don't just want to go to a bowl game, I want to go to the best bowl there is and play for the Big 12 championship and the national championship.

"If you set limits for yourself, it makes it kind of tough. So there are no limits."

3

Tales from the
Missouri Sidelines

Giving the Tigers Their Roar

Dan Meers loved playing sports in his native St. Charles, Missouri, but he knew he could never compete at the collegiate level. So when he attended Mizzou from 1986 to 1990, he did the next best thing.

"At the end of my freshman year, I read in the student newspaper that they were having tryouts for Truman, the mascot," he said. "I thought, 'Well, that sounds interesting.' So I went to the informational meeting, and they talked about how you got to travel all over the country, and all you had to do was mascot the games. I tried out, and sure enough, I got the job. I had a great seat for four years in a row."

He also got a head start on his career. Today, Meers is better known as KC Wolf, mascot of the Kansas City Chiefs.

******

Being a football mascot during the late 1980s required a little creativity.

"They definitely weren't glory years for the Tigers, but I remember having a great time," Meers said. "For as poor as the football team played, the crowd still was a lot of fun. I remember getting down on the wall right by the track, acting like I fell backwards, and the fans all would catch me and pass me up over their heads. The security guards didn't like that one bit, so I had to

Truman the Tiger
(University of Missouri Department of Athletics)

pretend I had lost my balance or someone had pushed me so I fell backwards, and sure enough, they would pass me up the entire section.

"It never failed—there was always a policeman there to chew me out and tell me I wasn't supposed to do that. The good thing was, you're a mascot and are not supposed to talk. Sure enough, the next game I'd act like I fell over again, and they would pass me up again."

The Tigers were not much more successful on the road in those years.

"I remember we went to play in the University of Miami in the Orange Bowl—not the bowl game, but the stadium," he said. "I was just so excited to be able to go to Miami. We knew it was going to be hot, and sure enough it was in the mascot costume. I remember getting beaten 55-0 that day. We just got hammered, but I had a great time down there. I never dreamed one day I would wind up being a professional football mascot."

Meers became close to several football players.

"I remember a guy named Smiley Elmore," he said. "He had the biggest biceps of any human I had ever seen in my life. I also was an RA on campus and had several football players in my dorm, one of them named Larry Linthacum, who was a tight end. There were no real superstars, but the football players were some of the best-behaved guys I had on my floor."

******

The Tigers, however, were as successful on the hardwood as they were disappointing on the gridiron.

"The basketball games were always exciting," Meers said. "It was such an extreme to go from football to basketball, because you finally get to cheer for some winning teams. I was there when they cut down the nets for Big Eight championships."

University of Missouri president Elson S. Floyd, right,
is greeted by school mascot Truman the Tiger.
(AP/WWP)

******

Just like players and fans, Meers has fond memories of the Kansas rivalry.

"Those were some of the best games because of the atmosphere," he said. "I remember we played KU in Lawrence on an ESPN game and actually drove over from Columbia in a car. We were running late, and they stopped in front of Allen Fieldhouse. I ran through the door, found a changing room, and got there just in time for player introductions. That's the game I remember most, because I was sweating and thinking, 'Man, I'm going to be in big trouble.'"

******

Sparring with other Big Eight mascots was strictly an act, Meers said.

"Even though we acted like we got into it, we were pretty good friends," he said. "We used to do the Big Eight tournament in Kansas City each year, and I still have photos of Truman Tiger with a Jayhawk head on or Truman Tiger with Chip the Buffalo's head on. We would mix and match body parts and take pictures."

******

One road game in particular stands out.

"I remember we made a trip out to UNLV when they called it the Shark Tank with Jerry Tarkanian," he said. "That was back when they were highly ranked, and we went in there and actually beat them. That was a lot of fun, because I got to fly on the team charter."

The charter was a big deal, because Truman usually goes by bus. Perhaps the only thing worse than grueling bus rides is taking those rides while carting around a Tiger costume.

"Most of the trips I took were with the pep band and cheerleaders, and we got on buses and rode for hour after hour," Meers said. "I played more Uno in college on bus rides. I remember playing up in Madison Square Garden in the NIT and how long that bus ride to New York was.

"I never slept too good on those buses. I was one of the guys who didn't mind getting dirty and lying down on the floor, because I was tall and needed a place to stretch my legs. I actually slept really well in the aisle of the bus. The trouble was, when anybody got up to use the bathroom, there was a really good chance you would get stepped on two or three times a night.

"People still harass me about how bad you smell when you're a mascot."

******

Truman got to fly again when the Tigers played in the Maui Classic in Hawaii.

"That was a great trip, even though it was extremely hot over there," Meers said. "The games were played in small gymnasiums, nothing compared to the Hearnes Center. There was only one little fan in the corner. I think we played Louisville, and both mascots both were standing over there by the fan, trying to get as much air as possible.

"I got a grass skirt that said 'Truman the Tiger,' and the day after we played that game, I made the front page of the Maui newspaper. I made sure to clip that out and take it home with me for my scrapbook."

******

Kids from across the Show Me State proudly sported Band-Aids during the late 1980s.

"I remember Derrick Chievous and his Band-Aid," Meers said. "We would always try to put a Band-Aid on the Tiger's nose or something, because that was the big thing for the game."

******

Even a lovable mascot needs to know how to read the mood of the head coach.

"Norm Stewart was a character," Meers said. "We actually got along good, but I made sure to stay out of his way. He's intimidating, and it worked on me at that point. If there is anybody I didn't want to make mad, it was Norm."

Norm Stewart celebrates in 1998 during a Big 12 matchup with Oklahoma.
(AP/WWP)

Hall of Fame Perspective

Bob Broeg first set foot on the University of Missouri campus in 1936, which was Don Faurot's second year as head coach. Even after retiring from a stellar career as a sportswriter for the *St. Louis Post-Dispatch*, Broeg remains a fixture in the press box on football Saturdays. He has witnessed the great—and not-so-great—moments in Mizzou football for more than half a century.

"I saw only one game ever from the stands," he said. "My freshman year, I paid to see a game, then wound up working for the sports publicity department, and I never saw a game from the stands again. To this day, even though I buy four tickets, I sit in the press box, because I'm spoiled."

******

Broeg and Faurot forged a relationship that continued up until the former coach's death in 1995.

"I asked Don to write something for my autobiography, *Memories of a Hall of Fame Sportswriter*," Broeg said. "Faurot had just come back from Hawaii, and I got him on the phone and asked him. I never will forget his reply—it sent a chill through me. He paused and said, 'Bob Broeg is the finest journalist I've ever met.' I said, 'I want to cry.'"

Broeg had the opportunity to return the favor by writing an inscription on the Faurot statue that stands outside Faurot Field.

"They were just going to put 'Don Faurot, date of birth, date of death,'" he said. "I said to John Kadlec, 'John, shortly they will be calling him Fa-ROT. Let me write something about him.' I was very fond of what I wrote for the base of the statue. Faurot was a remarkable figure."

******

Broeg also has favorite memories of Faurot's successors.

"I was a real Dan Devine man," he said. "I wrote a foreword for his book, and it was so long that they made an epilogue out of it."

******

Broeg learned a memorable lesson about putting his faith in both Faurot and Devine. It came in 1959, when Faurot was athletics director and Devine was the second-year head coach.

"I saw Faurot overscheduling for money and getting beaten by close margins a lot of times," he said.

"The old near-miss. In 1959, Missouri was playing Michigan at Michigan, and Missouri was leading all the way. But then Michigan kicked a field goal that put them ahead by 14-12, and I blew my stack. Faurot was sitting in the second row with Fritz Kreisler. I said, 'These near-miss games!'

"Then Missouri, playing with a second-string quarterback because of the limited substitution rule, drove all the way and scored with two seconds to go. Missouri won. Faurot looked at me and said, 'Ye of little faith!'"

The story didn't end there.

"I made the mistake of telling that to Devine, and of course he got a big laugh," Broeg said. "So years later, after his Notre Dame team won an upset in the Cotton Bowl, he sent me a wire saying, 'Ye of little faith!' The irony was, I was going to watch all of the bowl games, but I had told my wife I needed to take a nap during the Cotton Bowl game, because Notre Dame would get beaten."

******

Several Nebraska games in particular remain etched in Broeg's memory.

"Missouri beat Nebraska in 1925, 1926 and 1927, but then they hadn't beaten them in the 11 years following a 7-6 upset in 1927," he said. "In 1938, I was in the press box in Lincoln, and Fred Ware, the sports editor of the Omaha *World-Herald*, asked Jake Campbell of the St. Louis *Globe-Democrat*, 'What about this Paul Christman fellow?'

"Several plays later, Christman threw a touchdown pass, and Campbell said, 'There he is, Fred.' Missouri won, 13-10, and Ware fell in love with Christman. He nicknamed him 'The Merry Magician.'

"The following year, I was with the Associated Press in Columbia, and this was Missouri's 100th anniversary as a university. The Columbia *Tribune* office was downtown, and I had a little cubbyhole in the window. Assistant coach Phil Bengston, later the coach of the Green Bay Packers, took the Catholic players to mass, and despite the fact they would play at 2:30, they would have a private lunch down the street—peaches, tea and toast, which is a good meal for quick elimination.

"He knocked on the window. I waved, turned to my typewriter and the next thing you know, he walked through the screen door and tapped me on the shoulder. He said, 'Hey, kid, I'll give you a big scoop. I'm going to pass the bums out of the stadium.' Christman threw three touchdowns by the half as Missouri beat Nebraska 27-13. It was the only defeat for Nebraska for two years.

"I always thought that game was most significant, because later on, after Missouri squeaked by Oklahoma in the rain, 7-6 to win the championship, then Nebraska shut out Oklahoma."

******

As fond as Broeg is of Mizzou football history, he doesn't dwell in the past. He believes quarterback Brad Smith will be remembered as one of the best to ever wear the black and gold. As a freshman in 2003, Smith became only the second quarterback in NCAA history to rush for 1,000 yards and pass for 2,000 yards in the same season.

"Even with my diminishing eyesight, I saw Brad Smith," he said. "Brad Smith, to me, was instantly the most poised newcomer since Paul Christman. His poise was superior."

******

Broeg's first wife died in 1975. The woman who would become his second wife asked her brother, a football coach, what he knew about Bob Broeg. The brother replied, "All I know is that he is in love with the St. Louis Cardinals and Missouri football."

There are worse ways for a man to be remembered.

Appendix 1

The Hearnes Center

A new $75 million dollar arena will replace the Hearnes Center in 2004.
(AP/WWP)

No Place Like Home

The Hearnes Center has been home to some of the greatest moments in Missouri basketball for more than three decades. It will give way to a new $75 million arena just south of Hearnes for the 2004-05 season.

The Warren E. Hearnes Multipurpose Building, as it is officially named, was dedicated by Gov. Warren Hearnes during summer commencement ceremonies on August 4, 1972. It has a seating capacity of 13,545 for basketball and cost $11 million to build. The building also has a 22-yard, eight-lane indoor track; a regulation-size practice basketball court; and practice areas for wrestling and gymnastics.

Here are a few records from the Hearnes years:

Record Home Crowds

Rank	Att.	Opponent	Date
1.	14,098	Kansas	January 22, 2000
2.	13,782	Indiana	December 7, 1999
3.	13,706	Kansas	February 11, 1989
4.	13,645	Iowa State	January 14, 1989
5.	13,610	Kansas	February 27, 1988
6.	13,558	Oklahoma State	February 21, 1988

Team Records at Hearnes

Longest Winning Streak:
34 (January 3, 1988 to December 8, 1990)

Most Points:
129 (December 30, 1987 vs. Alabama State)

Most Field Goals:
54 (December 30, 1987 vs. Alabama State)

Most Three-Point Field Goals
17 (December 6, 2001 vs. Southern University)

Most Free Throws
42 (December 8, 1976 vs. UTEP)

Most Rebounds
68 (January 12, 1976 vs. MacMurray)

Most Personal Fouls
32 (January 25, 1975 vs. Iowa State)

Appendix 2

Basketball Greats

Great Players, Great Memories

Hundreds of athletes have played basketball for Ol' Mizzou, but only six have been honored by having their numbers retired. Ironically, their names all begin with the letter "S."

Doug Smith (#34) Smith was only the third player in conference history to score more than 2,000 points and grab more than 1,000 rebounds in his career. He earned numerous honors, including being named an All-American and Male Athlete of the Year in the Big Eight. The Dallas Mavericks made him the No. 6 overall pick in the draft.

Willie Smith (#30) "Mr. Magic" led the Tigers to their first conference championship in the Norm Stewart era in the 1975-76 season. His scoring average that season, 25.3 points per game, is still the highest in school history. Perhaps his finest moment was scoring 43 points against Michigan in NCAA Midwest Regional final when the Tigers fell just short of reaching the Final Four.

Bill Stauffer (#43) Stauffer was a standout performer in the early days of Missouri basketball, from 1950 to 1952. He ranked 15th in the nation in rebounding as a junior and 11th as a senior. In his three seasons, he grabbed 964 rebounds, a mark that would stand for three decades.

Norm Stewart (#22) The legendary coach first was an All-American in 1956 after a senior season in which he led the Big Seven in scoring at 24.1 points per game. He also pitched for Missouri's 1954 College World Series Championship team. As head coach, he compiled 634 victories at his alma mater.

"Stipo," Steve Stipanovich (#40) Perhaps the most highly touted recruit in the history of the program. He left Mizzou in 1983 as the school's all-time leading scorer, with 1,836 points. In his senior season, he was a consensus All-American, as well as a first-team Academic All-American.

Jon Sundvold (#20) The smooth-shooting guard led the Tigers to four consecutive conference titles from 1980 to 1983. He twice earned All-Big Eight honors and was named an All-American in his senior season, when he averaged 17.1 points per game. He enjoyed a successful professional career with the Seattle Super-Sonics, San Antonio Spurs and Miami Heat.

Missouri All-Americans

1916	Fred Williams
1918-19	Craig Ruby
1920-21	George Williams
1922-23	Arthur Browning
1930	Marshall Craig
1931	Max Collins
1939-40	John Lobsiger
1952	Bill Stauffer
1956	Norm Stewart
1961	Charles Henke
1972-73	John Brown
1976	Willie Smith
1982	Ricky Frazier
1983	Steve Stipanovich
1983	Jon Sundvold
1987	Derrick Chievous
1990	Doug Smith
1992	Anthony Peeler
1994	Melvin Booker

Appendix 3

Faurot Field

M is for Memories

Memorial Stadium, home to Faurot Field, was built after coach Gwinn Henry won back-to-back championships in 1924 and 1925.

The giant "M" on the hill on the north end of Faurot Stadium is as much a part of Missouri lore as the Shack, "Beetle Bailey" and the columns. The M, made of whitewashed rocks, is 90 feet wide and 95 feet tall. In the 1950s, Nebraska fans turned the "M" into an "N" the night before the big game. The Mizzou groundskeepers enlisted some local boys to help restore the landmark in time for kickoff.

The playing surface itself has been changed several times. The old Omniturf, described as a skating rink by many players, was the playing surface when Colorado defeated the Tigers in the controversial "fifth down" game in 1990. Grass was reinstalled before the 1995 season; then the playing field was converted to Field Turf before the 2003 season.

The Tigers have drawn large crowds and set a number of impressive records in eight decades at Memorial Stadium:

Record Home Crowds

Rank	Att.	Opponent	Date
1.	75,298	Penn State	October 4, 1980
2.	75,136	Texas	September 29, 1979
3.	74,575	Nebraska	November 3, 1979
4.	73,655	Alabama	September 16, 1978
5.	72,348	Nebraska	October 15, 1983
6.	72,333	Colorado	October 18, 1980
7.	72,001	Nebraska	October 24, 1981
8.	71,291	Oklahoma	November 17, 1979
9.	71,096	Colorado	October 28, 1979
10.	70,915	Notre Dame	September 26, 1984

Team Records at Memorial Stadium

Most Consecutive Winning Seasons:
6 (1938-43)

Most Wins in Season:
5 (1960, 1969, 1974, 1980, 1981, 1983 and 1998)

Most Losses in Season:
7 (1985)

Most Consecutive Wins
19 (1938-43)

Most Consecutive Losses
8 (1984-85)

Undefeated Seasons
14 (1926, 1927, 1936, 1939, 1940, 1941, 1942, 1945, 1948, 1960, 1962, 1969, 1974 and 1982)

Winless Seasons
5 (1932, 1934, 1955, 1985 and 1994)

Appendix 4

Football Greats

The Best of the Best

The names of Tiger greats whose numbers have been retired span the generations:

Paul Christman (#44) "Pitchin' Paul" rewrote the Mizzou passing record book from 1938 to 1940, and many of those records stood for more than four decades. Christman, an All-American in 1939 and 1940, was the first Tiger to be inducted into the National Football Foundation Hall of Fame.

Darold Jenkins (#42) Jenkins was a center and linebacker for the Tigers in 1940 and 1941. He was named to 17 All-America teams and inducted into the National Football Foundation Hall of Fame.

Johnny Roland (#23) Roland was a tenacious running back and a first-team All-American on defense. The well-rounded player from 1963 to 1965 went on to earn NFL Rookie of the Year honors with the St. Louis Cardinals.

Bob Steuber (#37) Steuber flourished in Don Faurot's Split-T formation, running for 2,030 yards between 1938 and 1940. He still holds the school record for most points scored in a season, 121.

Roger Wehrli (#23) Roland and Wehrli shared both No. 23 and immense skills. Wehril, a consensus All-American in 1968, also was the leading punt returner in the nation. He later became a perennial All-Pro defensive back for the St. Louis Cardinals.

Kellen Winslow (#83) Winslow is widely regarded as the best tight end ever to play the game. In 1978 alone, he caught 28 passes for 479 yards and six touchdowns. He was a two-time All-Big Eight selection and a consensus All-American as a senior.

Missouri All-Americans

Year	Player
1925	Ed Lindenmeyer
1939	Paul Christman
1941	Darold Jenkins
1942	Bob Steuber
1955	Harold Burnine
1960	Danny Larose
1961	Ed Blaine
1962	Conrad Hitchler
1965	Johnny Roland
1965	Francis Peay
1967	Russ Washington
1968	Roger Wehrli
1969	Mike Carroll
1973	Scott Anderson
1973	Johnny Moseley
1975	Henry Marshall
1976	Morris Towns
1978	Kellen Winslow
1980	Bill Whitaker
1981	Brad Edelman
1981	Jeff Gaylord
1983	Conrad Goode
1986	John Clay
1998	Devin West
1999	Rob Riti
2000	Justin Smith

Appendix 5

Bowls

Going Bowling

Year	Bowl	Opponent/Result
1924	Christmas Festival	Southern California 20, Missouri 7
1939	Orange	Georgia Tech 21, Missouri 7
1941	Sugar	Fordham 2, Missouri 0
1945	Cotton	Texas 40, Missouri 27
1948	Gator	Clemson 24, Missouri 23
1949	Gator	Maryland 20, Missouri 7
1959	Orange	Georgia 14, Missouri 0
1960	Orange	Missouri 21, Navy 14
1962	Bluebonnet	Missouri 14, Georgia Tech 10
1965	Sugar	Missouri 20, Florida 18
1968	Gator	Missouri 35, Alabama 10
1969	Orange	Penn State 10, Missouri 3
1972	Fiesta	Arizona State 49, Missouri 35
1973	Sun	Missouri 34, Auburn 17
1978	Liberty	Missouri 20, LSU 15
1979	Hall of Fame	Missouri 24, South Carolina 14
1980	Liberty	Purdue 28, Missouri 25
1981	Tangerine	Missouri 19, Mississippi 17
1983	Holiday	BYU 21, Missouri 17
1997	Holiday	Colorado State 35, Missouri 24
1998	Insight.com	Missouri 34, West Virginia 31